AF259422

BLACK LEGACY PRESS™

WWW.BLACKLEGACYPRESS.ORG

The Cameroons
By
Albert Frederick Calvert

ISBN: 978-1-63652-418-4

THE
CAMEROONS

Albert Frederick Calvert

PREFACE

ALTHOUGH the designs, which German philosophers conceived and German statesmen and strategists spent thirty years in perfecting, for the conquest of our Cape territories and the creation of a Greater Germany extending from the Mediterranean to Table Bay, are best illustrated and exposed by the defiantly defensive policy they pursued in South-West Africa, the rise, development and fall of the German Colonial Empire is more completely epitomised in the chapter dealing with the Cameroons.

The establishment of the German East African protectorate forms a story that is intensely interesting, inasmuch as it reveals the duplicity of Teutonic methods in their relations with native races, European rivals and their own agents. Bismarck, the last barbarian of genius, repudiated Dr. Karl Peters when, equipped with private capital and acting on his own initiative, he was acquiring in the hinterland of Zanzibar a well-watered, fertile province equal in extent to South Germany, and obtaining from the Sultan the concession for the ports of Dar-es-Salaam and Pangani. It was necessary in 1884 for Germany to assure England that the Imperial Government had no intention of securing possessions in a region which was admittedly within Britain's sphere of influence, and Bismarck pursued Dr. Peters to Africa with an official intimation that the State would not grant him protection for the lives of his party, or for any possessions he might acquire opposite Zanzibar. But when the intrepid Teuton, as the representative of the German East Africa Company, had accomplished the spade work and returned to Berlin, the Government continued negotiations with the Sultan through their Consul-General at Zanzibar. The formal ratification of the treaties made in the name of the Company, was followed by a revolt of the Arabs, and when the Company's representatives had been allowed to be murdered or put to flight, Bismarck was able to declare that the situation that had arisen was beyond the control of private enterprise, and an expedition, under Major von Wissman, was accordingly despatched to East Africa to suppress the slave traffic which still flourished in that region. For the furtherance of such a humane and civilising purpose, the co-operation of the British fleet was readily enlisted, and with this support and the energetic measures taken by von Wissman's army of ex-British native soldiers, the disaffected populace was eventually "pacified," even if the slave traffic was not suppressed. The Company's claims to the territorial concessions granted under the treaties having been made good—Great Britain could not, in politeness, protest against the acquisition of Mount Kilimanjaro, since the amiable Kaiser had expressed a sentimental wish that the highest peak in Africa might be within the sphere of German *kultur*!—the Reichstag voted ten and a half million marks for the maintenance and development of these newly acquired territories. Then, and not until then, did England realise that with the connivance of Downing Street and the assistance of British men-of-war, this rich and important territory, with an area of 384,000 square miles, had become a Protectorate of Germany. Having duped England, punished the natives, and established their rule, it was only necessary to recall Dr. Peters and hand him over to the tender mercies of his official and political enemies, to make this chapter of the history of German empire building characteristic in its completeness.

What Germany succeeded in doing in East Africa after years of intrigue and deceit, and the expenditure of much blood and money, she accomplished in the acquisition of Togoland with a minimum of cost or trouble. Dr. Nachtigal, in the capacity of German Trade Commissioner, was sent to West Africa by his Government to enquire into and report upon the progress of German commerce in those latitudes. He was despatched at a time when the English Government had completed their leisurely deliberations upon the appeal of the peoples of Togoland and the Cameroons to be taken under the protection of the British flag, and Mr. Hewitt, a British Consul, was voyaging to the Gulf of Guinea for the purpose of complying with the native request, when Nachtigal arrived there on his commercial mission. The German Commissioner, acting under instructions from the Imperial Chancellor, hastily unfurled the flag of the Fatherland at Lome, in Togoland, and succeeded in reaching Duala, and formally placing the Cameroons under German rule, before Hewitt arrived upon the scene. Lord Granville addressed a reproof to Bismarck for not having divulged the nature of the errand upon which Nachtigal had been sent, and the incident was closed. In the three decades that followed, the German administrators in Togoland, with the thoroughness with which the Teuton is gifted, taught the natives the "sharp lesson" considered necessary to prepare them for the reception of Germany's civilising rule, furnished the colony with 200 miles of railway, over 750 miles of excellent roads of native construction, a score of postal and telegraph stations, and a telephone system, and established a wireless station—the most powerful in the world outside Europe—which was not only in communication with Berlin, 3,450 miles distant, but with East Africa, the Cameroons and South-West Africa. The final installations at Kamina were completed in June, 1914; in August the German operators learnt by wireless that Great Britain had declared war on Germany; and on 26th August the Kamina Station notified Berlin that the colony of Togoland, the smallest, completest, and only financially independent German possession, had capitulated to an Anglo-French force.

The German annexation of South-West Africa was a more intolerably humiliating and provocative act of aggression; it is one that only now—after the territory has been recovered by the brilliant campaign of the Union Army under General Louis Botha—can be forgiven Lord Granville. Prior to 1883 the natives of Damaraland and Namaqualand, suspicious of the intentions of Germany, had petitioned to be taken under British protection. Downing Street experienced a temporary uneasiness, but Bismarck's assurance that Germany had no intention of establishing Crown colonies in Africa, extinguished the fleeting distrust. The Cape Colony was not so easily satisfied. A British Commissioner, who was appointed to confer with the native chiefs, reported favourably upon the proposal to officially confirm the authority of the Cape Government over the region extending northward from the Orange River to Portuguese Angoland. Sir Bartle Frere, the Governor of Cape Colony, urged upon the home Government the desirability of the step, and the Colonial Office decided upon the formal acquisition of the port at Walfisch Bay. Bismarck, hesitating to commit what might be construed as a deliberately hostile act, invited Great Britain to state her intentions with regard to the rest of the south-west territory, but failing to receive any definite reply, he decided upon bold if impudent measures, and in April, 1884, the Chancellor announced that the territory north of the Orange River was under the protection of the German Empire. As Bryden says, in his

History of South Africa, "it was an unfriendly act, carried out in an unpleasant manner, and the British Colonists in South Africa are not soon likely to allow it to pass out of remembrance." It not only destroyed the symmetry of a British South Africa, and gave Germany rights in territories marching with British colonies, but it added 322,450 square miles of African territory to the German Colonial Empire, for which a Bremen merchant named Luderitz parted with a hundred pounds and a score of old muskets.

Germany's method of developing her new possession in South-West Africa was entirely in keeping with her manner of acquiring it. From the first she proceeded to colonise on military lines. Railways were constructed with regard to their strategic importance; they were made on what is still called the Cape gauge; and were directed towards the Union border. A standing army was raised and compulsory service was instituted. An artillery depot established at Windhoek, the capital, contained a worthless collection of old gun-carriages and bales of locally-collected hay. This was to secure the colony against the imaginary evil intentions of the inoffensive and unarmed Ovambos, who inhabit the north-east corner of the colony. At Keetmanshoop, some hundreds of miles further from Amboland, but within 150 miles of Cape territory, was a great arsenal, furnished with guns and shells, rifles and cartridges, ambulances, transport vehicles, and military stores and supplies sufficient to equip and maintain an army of fifteen thousand men for two years. In the face of these facts and figures, we may be forgiven for doubting the honesty of the German Colonial Secretary's denial that Germany ever had any intention of occupying, either permanently or temporarily, the territory of the South African Union, and of disregarding the expression of Lord Haldane's pious belief that the Kaiser's life's purpose was "to make the world better," and that in Germany's method of colonial expansion, "she was penetrating everywhere to the profit of mankind."

In some ways the story of Germany's annexation of the Cameroon provinces, and her subsequent extension of that area, is the most interesting of all, because if she secured her footing in East Africa by subterfuge, and in South-West Africa by the exercise of sharp practice supplemented by a certain display of bold decision, she edged her way into the Gulf of Guinea by virtue of no other quality than that of sheer bluff, but, having consolidated herself in the positions she had thus gained in West Africa, she allowed the world to understand that she was determined to expand her sphere of influence, if necessary, by recourse to arms. In 1885 Germany legalised her occupation of the Cameroons by placating France with an exchange of unimportant territories, and renouncing in favour of Britain her nominal claims to St. Lucia and to Forcados, at the mouth of the Niger River.

Having thus solidified their position, and secured themselves against what Passarge calls "the intrigues and provocations of the English," the German administrators proceeded to Germanize their new province and systematically to develop its tropical resources. Although they established customs houses, courts of justice and post-offices, and constructed about 125 miles of a projected railway system of 285 miles, and, between 1898 and 1911, increased the total trade of the colony by nearly forty million marks, the colony did not prove a departmental or material success. The staffs of the Experimental Institute of Agriculture at Victoria and the Department of Agriculture at Buea, devoted their energies to the scientific raising of tropical economic plants, to experiments in plantation culture, and to the training of young natives in the virtues of Teutonic industry and organisation, while, by Government Proclamation, all native children were compelled to attend the Government schools, acquire an intelligent knowledge of the language and history of Germany, and practice the art of singing German patriotic songs. Despite this paternal concern for the agricultural and educational well-being of the natives, the application of German methods proved a disappointment. The children at the end of their school course considered themselves too superior to undertake manual labour, while the men, resenting the German indifference to their national feeling and inherited methods of work, developed the spirit of native unrest. A lack of sympathetic understanding of the natives was attended by culpably injudicious treatment of them by the German officials, and the relations between the authorities and the aborigines led to the frequent employment of the Imperial troops, while the inadequacy of means of internal communication rendered the progress of "one of the most productive countries in the world" both slow and difficult.

But, disappointing and costly as was the German failure to administer and develop the Cameroons, the Teutonic lust for territory was unabated, and, in its resolve to extend its holding in this quarter of the globe, the Government did not hesitate to emperil the peace of Europe. When the German cruiser *Panther* appeared at Agadir, in July, 1911, the object of the Wilhelmstrasse was not to protect purely imaginary German interests in that part of Morocco, but to maintain a menacing attitude that would compel the French to cede to the Bully of Europe their territory to the south of the German Cameroons. The negotiations for the transfer were concluded in June, 1913, and fifteen months later French and British troops commenced a joint expedition to wrest from the German authority, by military means, the province from which the former had been ejected by diplomatic blackmail and the insistant rattle of the sword in the scabbard.

It is instructive to recall the methods by which Germany acquired her African possessions, if only for the partial answer it provides to the question as to what the Allies intend to do with them. It is absolutely certain that however the Allies agree to dispose of the four colonies in question, they will never be restored to Germany, notwithstanding the fact that Herr Dernburg has committed the Emperor to the pledge that he will never consent to make peace except on terms which include their surrender. Germany got into Africa as a burglar effects an entrance into a well-stored building, but it is not because her gains were ill-gotten that she will be deprived of them. Having experimented in the civilisation of natives for three decades, she has revealed an utter inability to colonise for the benefit of mankind, but the hopeless failure of the German system of imposing her rule upon subject races, is not the reason why she will henceforth be debarred from participation in the work of civilising the world. The colonial possessions of Germany, as well as of England, France and Belgium, form part of the stakes for which all Europe is in arms, and they will become the spoils of the conquerors. As the Imperial Chancellor has announced, the future of the Cameroons will be decided not in West Africa, but in another theatre of war.

Germany's explanation of her desire to acquire colonies was based upon her need for extra territory capable of supporting her growing population. For this purpose she acquired East Africa, and immediately set about the task of raising, equipping and drilling a large force of black troops. She seized the French Cameroons, and at once increased the handful of natives which the French had found sufficient for the maintenance of order in the colony, to an army of 1,550 black and 185 white troops, and she had planned the formation of additional corps of mounted infantry, and the rearming of all the troops with modern rifles. As soon as wireless telegraphy became a practical means of communication, a wireless station was installed in Togoland which rendered the little colony of inestimable potential value from a military point of view, while in South-West Africa, the extent and completeness of her defensive and offensive preparations, is abundant proof that the real value to Germany of this territory lay in the proximity of the region to the Boer States, disaffected to Great Britain. "The land was not taken for *bona fide* colonisation," wrote the Rev. William Greswell over thirty years ago, "only as a *point d'appui*." Germany pushed forward her military preparations in East, West and South Africa, as she did in Prussia, because she had convinced herself of England's ultimate inability to hold India, Egypt and her colonial dominions. Her professors assured the Kaiser and his junker parasites, that the English had lost both "the qualities of creative genius in religion and the valour in arms of a military caste", that we had become "a timorous, craven nation, trusting to its fleet"; and that, while we had "failed to impress our dominion" on the chiefs of the Indian Tributary States, the colonies were "shivering with impatience under the last slight remnant of the English yoke."

Because of their arrogant attempt to put their theories and their conclusions to the test, the German people are being stripped of all their overseas possessions. They have already lost their South-West Protectorate and Togoland, and the Allies are now successfully engaged in crushing German resistance in Eastern Africa. It is not my purpose in this little book to follow the fortunes of the Allied troops; it will be time enough to write the story of the campaigns when the task is accomplished, and the future administrations of the colonies are in operation. My object in the following pages is to give the public the particulars about the Cameroons which I have collected not without the expenditure of a considerable amount of time and trouble. A natural desire to ascertain the nature of the difficulties that would have to be surmounted by the allied forces, and a desire to learn something of the natural resources and commercial potentialities of the territory that was about to be acquired, sent me to bookshops and libraries in search of works that would satisfy my curiosity. I was disappointed to find that the information I wanted was not available in English form, English authors having decided, apparently, that the colony did not lend itself to interesting or marketable compilation, and since the British Government had not accredited a Consul to the Cameroons, not even a belated Consular Report was procurable. In this extremity I turned my attention to such German publications as were obtainable in this country and, from the official writings of Dr. Paul Rohrback, Dr. Grotefeld, Dr. Paul Preuss, Dr. Walter Busse, Herr Eltester, and Siegfreid Passarge, I gathered a mass of information concerning the geographical and geological features, the vegetation and forestry, and the natives and native cultivation, together with an interesting summary of the progress made under the German system of development and the success they had attained in their experiments in plantation cultivation. In a paper written by Captain W. A. Nugent, R.A., who had been a member of the Boundary Commission in 1907, and acted as British Commissioner appointed to survey and fix the boundary between the German Cameroons and Nigeria in 1912, I found a full and admirable description of the territory traversed. This volume contains the result of my researches, selected and arranged in such a manner as will, I trust, be found acceptable to English readers who share my curiosity concerning the natural resources, the commercial position and the prospects of the colony, and who also entertain the hope that part of it, at least, will ultimately form a link in the chain of British overseas dominions.

ALBERT F. CALVERT.

Royston,
Eton Avenue, N.W.

CONTENTS

DISCOVERY AND EXPLORATION

THE large bay or estuary in the Gulf of Guinea, lying south of Nigeria and facing the island of Fernando-Po, was discovered by Portuguese navigators in the fifteenth or sixteenth century and christened the Rio dos Camaroes (the River of Prawns), from the abundance of Crustacea that infested its waters. The name was also used to designate the neighbouring mountains, which rise to the north-west of the bay. The English usage, until the end of the nineteenth century, was to confine the term, the Cameroons, to the mountain range, and to speak of the estuary as the Cameroon River. It was left to the acquisitive Germans to extend the use of the name in its Teutonic form—Kamerun—to the whole Protectorate.

The establishment of German trading firms and factories at various places on the West African coast suggested to the Imperial Chancellor the practicability of laying the foundations of his projected German Colonial Empire in the Cameroon region of the Dark Continent. On March 19th, 1884, Dr. Nachtigal, a former Consul at Tunis, was instructed to proceed on this civilising mission, and on July 5th and 6th he hoisted the German flag at Bayida and Lome, in Togoland. On the 10th of that month the English gunboat *Goshawk* entered the Cameroon River, and the mission's hope of further extending the sphere of German influence on the coast of West Africa appeared doomed to extinction. But the *Goshawk* departed on the following day, leaving the field clear for Nachtigal, who rushed through some agreements with the chiefs Deido, Bell and Akva, declared the country to be under the protection of Germany on July 14th, and appointed Doctor Buchner Provisional Governor of the newly acquired territory. The new Governor acknowledged the protest against German occupation, which was formally made by the British Consul on July 19th, and proceeded to hoist the German flag at Bumbia, Maliba, and Batanga.

In this nefarious and undignified manner the German Government obtained a foothold in the Gulf of Guinea, but it still remained for them to regulate their intrusion among the nations already established in the region. In order to solidify the position they had taken up, and, in the phrase employed by Siegfreid Passarge, "to withstand the intrigues and provocations of the English," who laid claims to Victoria and the Rio del Rey coast, it was necessary to have the treaty of occupation confirmed. On May 7th, 1885, a treaty was concluded by which the British waived their claims in favour of Germany, who reciprocated by renouncing their nominal claims to Forcados, at the mouth of the Niger, and to St. Lucia. In the same year the French ceded Great Batanga and the island west of Kwakwa-Kriek in exchange for the German possession of Konakry. These treaties legalised the position, and Germany was left a free hand to develop her possessions in the Cameroons, under the Governorship of Baron von Goden.

In July, 1911, the German cruiser *Panther* appeared off the coast of Morocco, at Agadir, for the alleged purpose of protecting German interests, of which no trace existed in that quarter of the globe. The incident was ultimately closed by the cession to

Germany of the French territory to the south of their Cameroon colony, which was subsequently incorporated with it under the name of New Cameroon. The transfer was made in June, 1913. Under French domination, three military stations, garrisoned with a total force of four officers, twelve non-commissioned officers, and 200 native troops, had been sufficient to preserve order, but the new rulers had their own ideas as to the military requirements of their growing Empire. We read in *Jahrbuch über die Deutscher Kolonien* (1913) that the German defence force numbers 185 Europeans and 1,550 natives, while it was the intention of the Government to form an additional corps of mounted infantry, to establish a stud farm for the breeding of troop horses, and to arm all the troops with 98·3 carbines. Since the declaration of war in August last, Togoland has capitulated to the French and British, and the German Cameroons are now being systematically and successfully invaded by the allied forces. The political future of these territories is, as yet, undetermined, but however they may be ultimately allocated, German domination in West Africa, with its blundering mismanagement and bumptious militarism, is a chapter of colonial history that is closed for ever.

THE EXPLORATION OF THE INTERIOR.

Although the commercial activities of the tribes inhabiting the African Mohammedan empires, and the construction of trade routes connecting Senegal with the Red Sea, had opened up the Soudan to Europeans, the territory which since 1884 has been known as German Cameroon was practically unexplored at the beginning of the nineteenth century. In 1822 an English expedition succeeded in reaching Lake Tchad and exploring its western and southern boundaries. This discovery was supplemented in 1851-52 by Barth and Overweg. Barth went from Kuka to Yola, and discovered the upper course of the Benue. He penetrated further, through the country south of Lake Chad to Bagirmi. In 1854 Baikie went up the Benue, as far as Djen, about fifty kilometres from Yola. Rohlf's journey in 1865-67 and Nachtigal's in 1869-74 are of little importance. In 1879 began the activity of Edward Flegel, who, on the steamer *Henry Benn*, navigated the Benue as far as Garna. Of much greater importance were the explorations of the Benue district in 1882 and 1883, the southern limit of which was marked by the towns of Ngaumdere, Banjo, Gaschaka, and Takum.

The knowledge of the coastal district was extremely limited. Burton and Mann had ascended the Cameroon mountains in 1861-62. In 1872-75 three German scientists, Buchholz, Reichenow and Lüders, made important zoological discoveries, while Rogozinsky, a Pole, in 1883, reached as far as Lake Barombi. But all efforts to penetrate into the interior were frustrated by the impracticable condition of the roads, the unhealthiness of the coast district—which was for the greater part uninhabited virgin forest—and by the hostile attitude of the natives.

After many fruitless endeavours to explore this coastal region, an expedition in 1888 succeeded in crossing from Batanga by way of Njong and Sanaga, and in settling the boundary between Bantio and Sudannegern. The effort to reach the Cameroon estuary was frustrated by the opposition of the Bakoko; and after a journey of much difficulty the expedition returned to the coast. In 1899 a station was established and a foothold secured. In the same year the region north of Duala was explored, and the forest district traversed, the plateau of Baliland was ascended, and the grassy lands reached. With indescribable difficulty the districts from Ibi on the Benue to Yola were traversed. In 1902-4 an Anglo-German expedition, after a very minute survey, fixed the boundary line between Yola and Lake Chad, and in 1908 an agreement was made between Germany and France regarding the south and east boundaries. In 1907-8 the frontier between Cameroon and the Nigerias was surveyed by the British and German representatives, and the approximate line of demarcation subsequently settled between the two Governments was fixed and marked by an Anglo-German commission in 1912-13.

BOUNDARIES AND TOWNS.

The Cameroons are bounded on the north-west by Nigeria, on the north-east and east by the French possessions of the Military Territory of Chad and the Middle Congo and the French possession of Gaboon. The frontier runs in a north-easterly direction from near Calabar in the Southern Provinces of Nigeria to Lake Chad, and then in a general south-south-east direction to about lat. 2° N., from whence it strikes south-west by west, reaching the Atlantic just south of Spanish Guinea, which is thus surrounded on the north, east and south by German territory. The general outline of the country thus described is broken in the middle east by a triangular piece of land which gives access to the Ubangi river, an affluent of the Congo, at Singa, in lat. 3° 40′ N.; whilst in the south-east corner a strip of land seventy miles broad runs southwards, giving access to the Congo itself in about lat. 1° S.

The Protectorate, with an area of 290 square miles, had

in 1913 an estimated native population of 2,650,000, and a European population of 1,871, of whom 1,643 were Germans.

The chief towns on the coast, from north to south, are Victoria, Duala (the capital), Kribi, and Ukoko. Buea is a large town on the eastern slopes of the Cameroon mountain, and Edea is on the Sanaga, about forty miles from its mouth. In the mountainous region in the north-west are Bare, Dschang, Bali, Bamenda, Wum, Esu, and Kentu; to the east of these is Fumban, and to the west, in the low-lying country near the Nigerian border, Ossidinge. In the western portion of the plateau are Tibati, Banyo and Tingere, and in the centre, at the junction of the main routes of the interior, is Ngaumdere. In the country north of the plateau the chief towns are Garua, an important trading centre on the Benue, Lere, Binder, Marua, Mora, Dikoa, and Kusseri. In the southern part of the country are Yaunde, Dume, Bertua, Gaza, Carnot, Bania, Lomie, and Akoafim. Molondu is in the extreme south-east.

THE PROGRESS OF THE PROTECTORATE.

In the first twenty-eight years of their occupation the Germans had established courts of justice at Buea, Duala, Kribi, and Lomie, custom houses at Duala and Buea, thirty-eight post offices throughout the territory, and had maintained order among the natives by means of twelve companies of Imperial troops. They had constructed and opened 108 kilometres of the 1-m. gauge line of 160 kilometres from Duala to the Manenguæ Mountains, and had opened the central line from Duala to Widimange, on the Nyong River—a distance of 293 kilometres of 1-m. gauge line—as far as Edea, ninety kilometres from Duala. The imports had increased from 9,296,796 marks in 1898 to 29,317,514 marks in 1911, and their exports in the same period had risen from 4,601,620 to 21,250,883 marks, a total increase in the trade of the colony of nearly thirty-seven million marks. The want of means of communication was found a hindrance in the economic development of the territory, which was admittedly possessed of "unlimited liabilities." Vast tracts in the interior were proved to be suited for cotton cultivation; oil palms, cocoa, and rubber were ascertained to be of "incalculable wealth," and the Cameroons were described by Dr. Grotewold as among the most productive countries in the world.

But the administration, or the critics of the administration of the Protectorate, had discovered that the lack of proper means of communication was not the only factor that retarded the progress of this richly endowed country. The unrest amongst the natives had revealed on the part of the authorities the lack of that sympathetic understanding of their native subjects which makes for successful colonisation. Their treatment of the natives was culpably injudicious, and their mistakes in dealing with them were so frequent and serious that the relations between the Government and the native population were constantly strained, and the services of the Imperial troops were in great demand.

GEOGRAPHICAL AND GEOLOGICAL FEATURES.

The country on the whole is mountainous and forms the north-west limit of the central African plateau. The coastland is flat alluvial country spreading out on either side of the Cameroon Mountains, and broken up with mangrove swamps, lagoons and deep estuaries. The Rio del Rey region on the west of the

Cameroon Mountains is a stretch of alluvial land with a breadth of thirty to forty kilometres, which forms the extreme eastern portion of the great alluvial plain extending from the Gold Coast to the Cameroon, and attaining its greatest development in the Niger Delta. Within the alluvial the volcanic massive of the Cameroon Mountain rises to a height of 4,070 m., and divides the land into two parts, which are connected only by a small and high strip of territory. To the east of the dividing mountain lies Dualaland. The other three orographical regions which comprise the Cameroon country includes the Cameroon plateau, which forms the largest and most important part of the colony; the enormous region of Adamana, which is generally level and nowhere reaches an elevation of more than 600 metres; and the extensive swampy lands of the Lake Chad basin which are under water during several months of the year.

The greater part of the colony is covered with red, loamy, sandy weatherings, which are characteristic of the tropics. If this red earth contains hard concretions of brown iron ore, they are named "Laterit." These cellular-like volcanic scoria are characteristic of the surface of the soil generally, and especially in those districts where the loamy deposits have been washed away by heavy rains. Vegetable soil is more abundant in the rainy regions of the south, and also in the lowlands. Indeed the result of this humid weathering is a kind of whitish yellowy kaolin, or china clay, which is found in the south plateau. A blackish mould to a thickness of one or two feet covers the lowland south of Lake Chad, and is there called "Firki." Whilst in the south of the colony red and yellow clayey soil preponderates, the further north one goes to the dryer regions, reddish sand, a product of the physical weathering, is to be found.

CLIMATE.

In the coast region of the Cameroons the climate is warm and moist, with a high rainfall. The temperature is not excessively high, the heat being tempered by the cold Benguela current coming northward from the Polar regions. According to Knox (*The Climate of Africa*) February is the warmest month and July the coolest, the maximum and minimum temperatures being 89·7° F. and 66° F. respectively. The mean temperature at Victoria and Duala is about 77° F. The coast is one of the most unhealthy places in Africa, but the conditions are considerably better and more suited to Europeans in the high-lying districts in the north. The climate of the latter is largely of the continental type, characterised by extremes of temperature. At Bali the mean temperature is about 64° F., the maximum 87° to 90° F., and the minimum 43° to 45° F. At Fort Crampel, on the eastern side of the plateau, the maximum temperature reaches 113° F., and the minimum 49° F. On the Ngaumdere plateau it is sometimes very cold, and sleet storms are not uncommon, the temperature sometimes falling to 37° F.

As regards rainfall, there are as a rule four more or less distinct seasons in the southern and central regions—the chief dry season at the beginning of the year, the so-called long wet season from June to September, a short dry season in October and November, and a short period of great rainfall in part of November and in December—but the divisions indicated are by no means well marked. The Adamana district, situated on the north of the plateau, lies beyond the equatorial beet, and there are consequently only two seasons, one wet and one dry.

The massive of the Cameroon Mountains presents a district

which is singular with regard to its climate, vegetation and animal life. At its base is a primeval forest, and the climate is tropical and humid. Debundja and Bibundo have practically no dry season, the rain being continuous nearly the whole year round. On the east side, the rainy season lasts for only two to three months in the year. Buea, which lies on the lower slopes of the misty region, has a fresh, cool climate, and is quite free from malaria. The temperature varies frequently, in some cases from 1·5° to 2° Cent. in the course of two or three minutes. Instead of the usual heavy tropical rains, it has only a drizzling rain, and the humidity penetrates everywhere, even the dwellings. On the upper slopes, when the north-east wind blows, it is icy cold, except at midday. Hoar frost is frequent and snow fairly so. The mountain is nearly always cloud-capped, and it is seldom possible to obtain a really clear view of the summit.

VEGETATION AND FORESTRY.

The combination of tropical heat and rain in the alternate regions of forests and brushwood swamps produces a tropical growth of cocoa palms, cotton plants, flax and fibrous trees, and rubber vines in prodigal luxuriance and variety. The virgin forests are tropical to a height of about 1,000 m., when they become less dense, and the oak ferns make their appearance. Between 1,500 and 1,800 m. the wild coffee shrub grows abundantly, the oak ferns disappear, and are succeeded by glades and brushwood. At an altitude of 2,200 m. the forest suddenly comes to an end and the grass land begins. Only in the ravines, in which the soil is moist and sheltered from the winds, the forest continues to the 2,700 m. level. The high forest—the most magnificent of all tropical forest formations—is characterised by its amazing variety of entirely different trees, including, among others, the great wool tree, the mahogany tree, the yellow and red wood trees, the oil-palm, and rubber. Among the trees of the brushwood districts the principal are acacias and the oil-palm, which to a height of from 700 to 900 m. covers the slopes of the Cameroon plateau to the coast.

The chief planting activity appears to have been at Johann-Albrechts-Höhe, and in the Dibombari district on the Northern Railway. A forestry plantation at Manoka, near Duala, was abandoned on account of its remoteness, the difficulty of water supply, and the constant lack of labour. The principal work for the making of forest and state reserves has been conducted in Yabassi, Yaunde, Edea, and Dschang. The efforts of the forest department and of private persons have been concerned mainly with: (*a*) Investigations of woods suitable for beams, wharves, and for boat and waggon building; (*b*) trials of woods resistant to *teredo navalis* for small boats; and (*c*) experimental shipments to German South-West Africa of woods serviceable for building, mining and street paving.

A large increase, amounting to 270 per cent. in the production of building and other timber, took place in 1911. The first place in the exports is held by Cameroons mahogany, which is stated to be increasing gradually in value in the market; its exports having risen in value from £7,022 in 1910 to £22,000 in 1912. The next wood in importance is Cameroons ebony, the exports of which have been as follows: 1909, 672 tons, worth £3,038; 1910, 1,221 tons, worth £6,090; 1911, 1,652 tons, worth £6,777; whilst in 1912 the value of the shipment was £9,055. The increase of exports has been largely due to an increase of cutting by the natives, and this has entailed a considerable amount of robbery by them. As a consequence, timber exploitation on Government lands was entirely prohibited to natives in the period 1912-13, and concessions were given to Europeans with much caution; a decrease in the production was therefore expected. A difficulty regarding the exploitation of timber in the Cameroons is the lack of good waterways in the forest regions.

CATTLE RAISING.

In spite of the very great difficulties caused by the tsetse fly, much attention has been paid to stock-breeding in the Cameroons, although with the exception of certain efforts made in Kusseri, in the extreme north, and in Garua, in Adamana, nothing in the nature of methodical horse-breeding by natives exists. The indigenous cattle are of two kinds, the dwarf cattle and the humped cattle. Cattle-breeding in the proper sense is only found among the Fulla tribe in Adamana, in Banyo and the Lake Chad regions. From these places there was once an active export of cattle to the neighbouring British and French Protectorates, but this has been diminished in recent years owing to a large export duty. The interest in cattle-production on the part of the natives has been increased in recent years, under official encouragement, in the districts of Dschang and Bamenda.

The Fulla cattle are greatly prized in the central districts, in which, by reason of the ravages of the tsetse fly, no cattle can be bred, and when railway communication has cleared the infected regions, a thriving cattle export industry to the coast will be developed. The increased prosperity of the rubber districts of the south, especially Molondu, Dume and Lomie, has led, in recent years, to a demand for meat among the natives, and this has been supplied from the Hausa and Fulani herds. In 1911 about 20,000 head of large stock and 8,000 of small stock were sent from Adamana to the south, and this is estimated to mean an exchange between the north and the south to the value of about £150,000.

As is usual in West Africa, the natives possess neglected goats, sheep and fowls, and in some cases pigs, though this is only true to a very small extent in the southern districts.

NATIVE AGRICULTURAL PRODUCTION.

The chief agricultural products of the Cameroons are rubber, palm kernels, cocoa and palm oil, and the Protectorate may be said, in a general way, to present three chief agricultural areas: the southern, with rubber in increasing production; the middle province around the Cameroon river basin, with their plantations and areas rich in oil palms; and the grass country, northward, suited specially for cattle breeding. Nearly all the rubber exploited has been derived from the native exploitation of wild plants. Almost all the male population of Lomie, Molondu, Dume, and Dengdeng was concerned in rubber collection in 1910-11, in which years more than 1,000 coloured middlemen bought the rubber from the natives and sold it to the forty-nine mercantile firms who had no fewer than 230 stations established for its purchase. The comparatively small share of rubber plantations in the whole production of the Protectorate is shown by the fact that, of a total export of 5,957,516 lbs. in 1911, all except 23,912 lbs. was from wild plants; whilst in 1912 cultivated plants accounted for only 53,040 lbs. in a total shipment of 6,184,222 lbs. The results of the attempts to induce the natives to take up new cultivations depend on the presence or absence in their district of wild plants that they can exploit. Whilst, for example, the inhabitants of the Lomie district, who still know of rich stands of wild rubber plants, are hardly to be excited to commence rubber cultivation, it has been experienced in Kribi, where these do not exist, that the distribution of young plants are gratefully received and readily planted.

It is also recorded that oil-palm cultivation has been introduced with some success to the natives, in the districts of Lomie and Yaunde, but any "cultivation" by the natives is very simple in nature, consisting merely in the keeping of the stands clear of "bush." The large decrease in the exports of ivory in recent years is due in great measure to the exhaustion of the stores of ivory hoarded by the natives and the extent of elephant shooting in the past ten years. The exports in 1910 amounted to sixteen tons, valued at £124, and although there was a slight increase of quantity in the following year, the export in 1912 showed a large diminution. The other native products are chiefly djair nuts, shea nuts, kola, and gum arabic, but there has been comparatively little activity as regards the actual cultivation of crops, because of the natural richness of the country in products which enable the inhabitants to buy what they require. The raising of food crops exists, however, for special demands, such as arise near railways, administrative stations and larger towns, and the chief places on the caravan routes and rivers. Near such places the native raises maize, plantains, bananas, cassava, sweet potatoes and ground nuts, as well as sorghum (dura or dari) in the northern districts, and some kola and sesame in isolated places. In several districts a certain amount of tobacco is planted; there is also some little fruit raising, notably in the villages of Ambam. In the highlands of Dschang, and in other places, such as Ebelowe and Yaunde, new crops, such as the English potato, "black bush" beans and turnips, for which the climate seems to be suited, have been introduced. Numerous inhabitants of the districts of Duala and Edea have in recent years laid out farms for the raising of cassava, plantains, maize, yams, and other products.

North of the watershed the principal crops are guinea-corn, millet, ground-nuts, cassava, and sweet potatoes; cotton and tobacco are also cultivated by the Chamba pagans, Zumperis and Munchis. The corn is planted in April at the end of the rainy season, the method of cultivation being as follows. The ground is first cleared of weeds and the remains of the last year's crop. It is then prepared for sowing by digging shallow trenches with a rough kind of hoe, the earth being piled up to form ridges between the trenches. Guinea-corn (*Sorghum vulgare*), the staple food of the country, is planted in these ridges. It grows to a great height, often fifteen to twenty feet, and is harvested in November. Millet is planted in the furrows; it ripens rapidly and is harvested in July. Cotton is ready for picking after December; tobacco and cassava are cultivated during the dry season on the hillsides, the streams being used for irrigation.

From October to March, during the dry season, the natives are engaged in stacking their corn into mud-walled granaries, and threshing what they require for immediate use. These months are also spent in repairing the damage done to the villages, grass being cut and tied into bundles for thatching roofs, and making new zana matting. The dry season is also the hunting season, when the long grass has been laid low by fire. This grass-burning is an annual institution, although the Government has given orders prohibiting it on account of the damage done to trees. But the hill tribes care very little for trees or grass, and a good deal for meat.

As in all parts where the tsetse fly prevails, and the employment of cattle for ploughing is impossible, the land is chiefly cultivated with the hoe; and as the West African hoe is a tool which calls for the exercise of patience rather than skill or strength, the native leaves the field work to his women. From this form of servitude the women will not be emancipated until cattle are rendered immune from tsetse fly and the hoe is supplanted by the plough.

PLANTATION CULTIVATION

T HE Cameroons were regarded by the Germans as a plantation country of the highest promise, and the proximity of the Cameroon Mountain to the coast, facilitating the realisation of the products, render this part of the colony an ideal area for the planter. All the largest plantations are situated in this district, which has been extensively developed, and its products have already assumed considerable proportions in the export statistics of the dependency. The laying out of a plantation in Cameroon is by no means an easy task, as the fertile soil must be drawn from the primeval forest. And as the Cameroon primeval forest has no equal for vastness and impenetrability, laborious and costly preliminary work is necessary before any real planting can be attempted. On the whole it is very much the same as in East Africa, with the distinction that as a rule in the latter colony there is only the so-called bush to clear, while in Cameroon one has to deal with high-grown primeval forest.

The cultivation of cocoa prospers on the slopes of the Cameroon Mountain, where the climate and soil resemble those of the adjacent Islands of St. Thomas and Fernando-Po, and its cultivation is almost confined to the Cameroon Mountain and to some plantations in Sanaga and Kampo. It is to be hoped that with the further opening up of the country, many districts will be found suitable for its cultivation. In this case the many years' experience on the Cameroon Mountain will facilitate the spreading. The cocoa-tree is, on an average, six to eight m. high, with a trunk diameter of about fifteen to twenty-five cm., and it begins to produce after four or five years. At harvest time the fruit must be carefully gathered, to avoid injuring the tree. The opening of the fruit to obtain the seeds is done with a cane, or by beating open the fruit on a stone. When the seeds are taken from the fruit, they undergo the important process of fermentation. It would take too long to relate the different methods employed, but it may be mentioned that the fermentation process affects the taste and aroma of the cocoa very much, drawing away the bitterness of the bean, modifying its sharp taste, and developing the aroma and the red-brown colour.

A still further proceeding is the drying of the beans, which is done either by the heat of the sun and the fresh air on threshing floors with removable roof, or by artificial heat in drying apparatus. Some days after the cocoa has been carefully dried, it is ready for exportation. It is packed in sacks or matting, and in the past it has been dispatched principally to Germany to be worked up in the factories. The kernels are ground and the grease when extracted is used in the form of cocoa-butter for medicinal purposes and for the fabrication of soap. The export of cocoa, which amounted to 2,450 tons in 1908, reached a total of 4,550 tons, valued at £212,500, in 1912.

RUBBER.

The attention of the rubber dealers was at first confined to certain lianas, especially the Landolphia florida, which was regarded as the greatest rubber-yielding plant in the colonies. But in the beginning of the century it was discovered that the great virgin forests of South Cameroon contained vast numbers of Kickxia-elastica trees, and that extensive subsidiary tracts covered with the same plant existed in the savannahs of South Adamana, in the Kumbo highlands, and the region of Lake Chad. Kickxia-elastica, known in the trade as "silk rubber," was first discovered on the West African Coast in Lagos in 1894, and by October of the following year the exports had reached well over a million pounds. The eagerness of the natives to exploit this very valuable product led to the total destruction of the rubber-yielding trees, with the result that by 1906 the export had entirely ceased. Dr. Schlecter introduced the Kickxia rubber trees from Lagos into the Cameroons, where he proved that 1½ lbs. of dry rubber may be obtained from the six-year-old trees, a result which was more than confirmed subsequently by Dr. O. Warburg, the well-known authority on rubber. The first shipments of rubber from the Kickxia trees were obtained from the wild rubber trees known as Funtumia-elastica, and it has only been during the last few years that the Germans, realising that the Kickxia rubber trees are indigenous to the colony, have cultivated it, and there are now large plantations of Kickxia in the Cameroons containing millions of trees, which are doing well.

From the tapping of wild Funtumia trees, it is known that this species yields latex more readily than others, and that it is almost as sensitive to drastic tapping as Castilloa. Tapping of the cultivated tree has occurred experimentally in Cameroon. These trees, however, do not stand closely-planted, but singly or in rows, and the results must be judged accordingly. It can be assumed that from 3 to 3¾ ozs. are to be expected from six-year-old trees planted at good distances from each other, and 1 to 2 ozs. from closely-planted trees. The method of tapping practised in the last experiments with Funtumia differed from all other methods, in that vertical incisions the whole length of the trunk were made. As to its advantage over the herring-bone system, further observations and a more extended series of comparative tapping trials are first necessary. The rubber is procured by boiling the latex after diluting it with water; treatment with hydrofluoric acid yields a better product. Although Funtumia rubber is at present inferior in quality to that of Hevea and Ficus, and at most is equal to that of the Castilloa, still it may be confidently anticipated that with more suitable preparation it will yield a good serviceable product.

THE COST OF PRODUCTION.

Most of the Kickxia plantations are laid out on land which has been cleared of jungle, a process which does not entail a heavy outlay. The expenses, including all costs for inspection, tools, labour, &c., amount to about £10 per acre. A fair supply of native labour is available, and the average wage, including board, is about £10 per annum. The cost of the upkeep of the planted areas should not exceed 30s. per acre for the first year, 22s. 6d. per acre for the second year, and 18s. 6d. and 10s. for the third and fourth years respectively. The estimated inclusive cost of tapping the trees and delivering the produce in Europe should not exceed 1s. 3d. per lb. The value of Kickxia rubber, if properly prepared, is almost equal to that of the best Para rubber, and it is certainly safe to estimate that it will always fetch within 1s. of Para. These figures compare very favourably with those obtaining in other plantations, and they are given here as an indication that in its rubber exports alone the Cameroon territory has a profitable future before it.

In considering the question as to whether Germany will ever be in a position to supply her own demands in rubber from her own colonies, Dr. Paul Preuss, writing in the *India Rubber Journal*, says that it depends on three factors: (1) Soil, (2) Climate, (3) Labour. "Regarding soil," he says, "the Colonies of Cameroon and New Guinea alone possess several hundred thousand acres of land suited for the cultivation of the most valuable rubber trees. The climate there is also very favourable. Taking the annual requirements of Germany in rubber at 16,000 tons, this quantity can be produced from an area of 150,000 to 170,000 acres exclusively planted with Hevea, and from 200,000 to 250,000 acres under cultivation with the various species already planted, but with Hevea predominating. Even if the demand for the raw material should considerably increase, the answer to this question would be an affirmative as regards soil and climate; whether, however, with the accompanying development in the cultivation of cacao, cotton, cocoa-nut and oil-palms, &c., the necessary labour will be procurable for such an extension in rubber cultivation, the question cannot be answered." It has been stated that in the coming years, when the rubber plantations are ready for tapping, and the tobacco plantations are demanding the services of thousands of natives, the insufficiency of labour will prove a serious problem, and the importation of Chinese labour was submitted to the consideration of the German Government as a feasible solution.

RICE, COFFEE, COCOA, AND TOBACCO.

During recent years the cultivation of rice has received more attention, especially in the experimental gardens. The forest land inhabitants have also begun to lay out water and hill rice fields in great extent, and it is only a question of time for the Cameroons to become a rice producing country. But whether the negroes will ever be capable of carrying out the troublesome cultivation of water rice, with the necessary transplanting and careful watering, is regarded as doubtful.

One can depend with greater confidence on the exportation of maize and millet from the forest land and the drier hinterland, as soon as means of transport are provided, as it has been found that the black can be entrusted with this cultivation. Rice, as well as maize and millet, and also bananas and pines, which grow in great quantities, would be, as native cultivation solely, open to question.

Regarding the cultivation of coffee, the greatest hopes were raised in the first years of occupation of the colony. The Cameroon Mountains resemble in every respect the island of San Thomé and Fernando-Po, where, in 1884, a flourishing coffee cultivation existed. Nothing was more natural than the expectation than that a fresh impetus would be given to coffee cultivation on the mainland, but these hopes were not fulfilled, and now scarcely any coffee plantations are to be found. Tea was planted in Buea by Deistel, and the tea-shrub developed splendidly.

Plantation cocoa has borne the preponderating share of the total exports of that product in recent years, the areas in bearing having increased as follows: 1909, 13,328 acres; 1910, 15,290 acres; 1911, 17,560 acres; 1912, 20,438 acres. The large increase of exports in 1912 is attributed to the very favourable weather in that year. It is stated that more care, with artificial manuring, is wanted in the cultivation, and that the chief diseases and pests of cocoa, such as brown rot, "cockchafer grubs," and "bark bugs," are not under control. Nevertheless the future for cocoa is believed to be good.

Much was expected of tobacco planting, especially in Bibundi, where tobacco was planted at first, and the quality was excellent, although the cultivation was proved to be too dear and too difficult on account of the dampness of the climate. In 1902 there was a deficit of 200,000 marks, and for some time the cultivation was discontinued. Attempts were made in 1911 to encourage tobacco planting in the German colonies by the guarantees of a definite price for quantities of at least 100 cwts. raised and prepared in those colonies. The planted area in plantations in the Cameroons increased from fifty acres in 1911 to 383 in 1912; 230 acres of the latter had yielded a crop. In view of the expensive nature of the cultivation, it was hoped that Cameroons' leaf for wrappers would gain a good market.

The planting of the Kola-nut was undertaken very energetically, and in 1904, 400 were planted in Garna, but with what result is unknown. The experimental cultivations in the gardens of Victoria have produced no palpable result. The trees flourished and bore fruit, but it was entirely consumed by worms. The natives, on the other hand, cultivate this tree in great extent in the forest land, and especially in the Kimbo highland. Among different plants, especially in the trial gardens, are the vanilla, pepper, nutmeg, cinnamon, and other spices. Vanilla was quite destroyed by blight in Victoria. Pepper, cloves and cinnamon all furnish excellent productions.

PALM OIL CULTIVATION.

The oil-palm in the old days was the glorious heritage of the native, who found a ready sale for such oil as his women-folk were able to extract by a slow and laborious process. It is likely that the native believed that so long as he retained the tree and the fruit, his time-honoured oil business would never be taken from him, but the great and growing demand for oil has beaten him, and he is fast losing the trade because he can no longer make the quantity that the market requires. Palm oil is now requisitioned for a hundred-and-one new uses. It is no longer the monopoly of the soap-maker or the chandler. Palm oil deodorised by hydrogen is needed for the "nut butters" of the vegetarian; makers of nitro-glycerine explosives derive their glycerine constituents more and more from palm oil; whilst the exploiters of novelties in metal polishes ransack the ship's hold for leakages from the palm-oil cask. Oil must be had in increasing quantity; machinery speeds up the production; yet still the cry is for more oil, until the European himself attempts to become owner of thousands of trees, eagerly and not too scrupulously encroaching on lands that once were considered native, in the vain hope of finding a speedier road to prosperity.

THE PALM TREE AND ITS PRODUCTS.

The profitable carrying on of this industry depends on the demand for palm oil and the use which can be made of the residues. That the supply of palm kernels themselves should decline is unthinkable. The steady increase in their growth in all parts of the West African Coast is conclusive evidence of their almost limitless possibilities. Moreover, the statistics clearly show the extensive nature of the demand. Great Britain and Germany are no longer the only purchasers; South Africa has entered the market, as well as Holland and France, though their lots are comparatively small, and could not in any way effect the profitable exploitation of kernel-crushing on a large scale.

In a paper read before the Royal Colonial Institute, entitled "The War: British and German Trade in Nigeria," Mr. R. E. Dennett, of the Forest Department, Nigeria, made it abundantly evident that Germany had been farming the commerce of the Protectorates to the detriment of the Britisher. He showed from statistics that Germany's export trade to Nigeria greatly exceeded ours, while of the Nigerian produce which left the country, Germany in 1913 took nearly all the copra, half the cocoa, more than two-thirds of the palm kernels, one-eighth of the palm oil, half the hides, one-third of the mahogany, more than half the ground-nuts, over a third of the shea nuts, and all the palm kernel cake.

On the subject of the palm tree and its products, Mr. Dennett is both interesting and instructive, and in view of its inevitable increase in importance as a British industry, the following extracts from his paper may be usefully reproduced here.

"People who have little or no knowledge of the palm tree

(*Elæis guineensis*) confuse the palm fruit with the palm kernel. The palm kernel of commerce is the seed of the palm tree. This is surrounded by a hard shell, and it is then called the palm nut. This shell is in its turn covered by an oily fibrous matter, and is then known as the palm fruit. If we take this fruit and cut it into two parts, we can see these three parts of the fruit more distinctly; first the outer yellow covering or the fibrous pericarp, from which the palm oil of commerce is extracted; then the shell, and finally the kernel, from which the white palm kernel oil is extracted.

"The composition of this fruit is as follows:—

Pericarp Oil	18	per cent.
Fibre and Moisture	12	"
Shell and Disk	58	"
Kernel	12	"
Total	100	"

"The uses of the palm oil tree are various. It yields the palm oil and kernels of commerce. It gives the native a drink he is very fond of, called palm wine, which, when fermented, gives our cooks yeast for bread-making. The shells of the nuts are used by blacksmiths as fuel, as they give off great heat. At the present time there are three methods of making palm oil: (*a*) from the fresh fruit, (*b*) from partially fermented fruit, and (*c*) from well fermented fruit.

THE NATIVE AS CULTIVATOR.

"Bunches of fruit having been severed from the parent tree, are sliced and hammered by natives, using long poles, until the fruit becomes detached from the bunch. The fresh fruit is either prepared at once into what is called soft oil, or allowed to ferment, or partially ferment, and made into hard oil. The procedure followed in making either of these kinds of oil is much the same. The fruit is placed either into canoes or clay troughs, water is poured over them, and then, by treading or beating, the fibrous matter containing the oil is separated from the nuts. The nuts are then taken out and placed in the sun to dry, while the fibrous matter, by further beating or treading, is made to yield the oil which floats to the surface of the water. This oil is ladled out into pots and boiled, and then allowed to rest, so that all dirt or sediment falls to the bottom of the pot. This clean oil, soft or hard, is the palm oil of commerce. This oil is taken in calabashes or tins to the traders' factory, which, generally speaking, is near to a river or a railway, and there put into casks and sent to the nearest port for shipment to Europe.

"There are, practically speaking, two kinds of palm oil exported from the West Coast, i.e., hard and soft, but soft oil is of two qualities—Lagos and ordinary soft oil. As a rule, Lagos and soft oil is worth £3 to £4 more than hard oil, the reason being that there is about 8 per cent. more glycerine in the soft than in the hard. The percentage of glycerine varies in inverse proportion with the acidity.

"In the olden days one of the chief occupations of slaves was that of cracking palm nuts; now this work is left to boys and women. After the nuts have been dried in the sun, they are heaped up under little sheds to protect them from the rain. In places where rocks are plentiful the nuts are taken there and cracked on them by a stone held in the hand of the cracker. In other places the nuts are put on a block of wood resting on the ground between the cracker's legs and struck with a piece of iron held in the cracker's right hand. In this way one worker will crack from 15 lbs. to 25 lbs. of kernels per day. The kernels are then packed in different kinds of baskets and taken to markets near rivers, where they are bought by native middlemen. Competition is very keen, and so these middlemen are tempted to adulterate the kernels by adding shells to them or by soaking them in water for two or three days. Finally, they are taken in canoes down rivers or by rail to the European traders and sold by measurement at so much a bushel.... Think of it! 241,000 tons of palm kernels shipped to Hamburg in 1913, and nearly every nut containing one kernel is cracked by hand."

THE FUTURE OF PALM OIL AND KERNEL INDUSTRY.

Although the palm kernel industry has not attained important dimensions in the Cameroons, there is no reason why it should not form one of the staple products of the colony, or why the whole of the trade in palm kernels should not be transferred from Germany to this country. Hitherto the quarter of a million tons of palm kernels—valued at over £4,000,000—exported annually from British West Africa has gone to Germany, where crushing-mills and manufacturing plants have been established, while considerable quantities of high-priced kernel oil, in manufactured or unmanufactured form, have been exported from Germany to Great Britain. About 50 per cent. of the produce of the crushed palm kernels is marketed in the form of oil, and the balance is made up into palm kernel cake, practically the whole of which is consumed in Germany, where it commands a good price and is in great demand, especially among dairy farmers.

This profitable German industry has now been suspended owing to the war, which has rendered it necessary for planters to find a new market for their produce, and the opportunity seems propitious for an endeavour to establish it in Great Britain upon a substantial scale. With a view to arousing interest in the subject in commercial and agricultural circles, Sir Owen Phillipps, K.C.M.G., Chairman of the West African section of the London Chamber of Commerce, has issued a timely pamphlet in which the present position of the trade is described and its potentialities are indicated. The Anglicisation of the industry, in addition to promoting Imperial commercial intercourse, and securing increased industrial employment in the United Kingdom, would furnish British farmers—who are complaining of the enhanced prices of present foods—with a new supply of a relatively cheap and excellent feeding material.

The profitable exploitation of this crushing industry depends upon the capacity of the British market to absorb a larger supply of palm kernel oil and upon the possibility of inducing British farmers to adopt the use of palm kernel cake. There are at present two mills, both at Liverpool, for dealing with palm kernels, capable together of crushing annually about 70,000 tons, leaving a balance unprovided for of at least 180,000 tons. To cope with this additional quantity several of the great milling companies of Liverpool, London, Hull, &c., have already made and are making alterations in their machinery in order to crush palm kernels, so that in the near future much greater quantities will be dealt with. A new mill on the Thames, at Erith, is also being erected, which, when completed after the war, will be capable of crushing a very large quantity.

PALM KERNEL CAKE FOOD.

In order to ascertain whether British farmers would be prepared to make a larger use of palm kernel cake, Sir Owen Phillipps placed himself in communication with the leading agricultural authorities in all parts of the country—principals of agricultural colleges, experimental stations, &c., and these gentlemen have taken up the matter with the greatest enthusiasm. They are practically unanimous in asserting that the fact of large quantities of palm kernel cake being available at a price comparing favourably with that of other similar foods (now becoming more expensive than formerly) has only to be brought to the notice of farmers to ensure a greatly increased demand; in fact, that farmers are looking out for a new and comparatively cheap feeding material. Many of the principals and professors of the colleges referred to in various parts of the country have undertaken an elaborate series of comparative experimental feeding tests with palm kernel and other cakes, so as to demonstrate the merits of the former. When these are completed the results will be made widely known to the agricultural community.

In an article published in the *Field* on "Palm Kernel Cake," Mr. F. J. Lloyd, F.I.C., points out that a really good cake, made from this product, is now available in this country. The nutrients in palm kernel cake are quite exceptionally digestible, and one German authority says that, "owing to its pleasant taste, its great digestibility, and the way in which cattle thrive on it, no cake fetches so high a price." It increases the yield of milk, improves the quality as regards butter fat, and is said to impart a good colour to the butter, so that it is especially valuable for winter feeding. Though mainly used in Germany for dairy cattle, Professor Lloyd adds that it has also been given with satisfactory results to steers, sheep, and pigs.

PALM KERNEL STATISTICS.

The *Bulletin* of the Imperial Institute contains an article calling attention to the magnitude of the trade in palm kernels, and discussing its commercial aspect. The following table shows the quantities and values from each of the chief producing countries in West Africa in 1912:—

	Quantities.		*Values.*	
	Tons.	*Tons.*	£	£
British Possessions:				
Gambia	445		6,518	
GoldCoast	14,629		205,365	
Nigeria	184,624		2,797,411	
Sierra Leone	50,751		793,178	
	———	250,449	———	3,802,472
French Possessions:				
Dahomey	36,708		535,937	
Gaboon	354		4,671	
Guinea	5,054		41,079	
Ivory Coast	6,692		70,710	
Senegal	1,736		28,221	
	———	50,544	———	680,618

Belgian Congo —		—	110,835
German Possessions:			
Kamerun	15,742		220,300
Togoland	11,456		168,978
	———	27,198	———	389,278
Totals		328,191	£4,983,203

This article also gives the average value of the kernels, which in Hamburg ranges from £18 2s. to £19 2s. per ton (June, 1914); the value in Liverpool was £17 17s. 6d. to £18 18s. 9d. per ton in July last, and in September was £16 7s. 6d. to £17 10s. per ton.

Palm kernel oil is used for the same purposes as cocoa-nut oil, viz., the manufacture of soap and candles and the preparation of various edible fats, such as margarine, cooking fats, vegetable "butters," and chocolate fats. By suitable treatment it can be separated into a liquid portion (olein) and a hard white fat (palm kernel stearin), and in this way the consistence of the material can be varied for the preparation of different edible products. These edible palm kernel oil products are prepared on a very large scale in Germany and elsewhere, and are largely imported into this country. With palm kernels at £17 to £18 per ton, the value of palm kernel oil in the United Kingdom is from £36 5s. to £36 15s. per ton, with Ceylon cocoa-nut oil at £40 per ton.

It is added that British oil-seed crushers who undertook to work them would find no difficulty in getting a market for the oil among soap-makers and makers of edible fats. Although the article points out that some difficulty might be experienced in finding a market quickly in the United Kingdom for the palm kernel cake, because English farmers do not readily take up feeding stuffs which are new to them, it will be gathered from what has already been said that, thanks to the initiative of Sir Owen Phillipps, this difficulty is likely to be overcome, and the opportunity is a particularly good one now that other feeding stuffs are becoming more expensive, as that is a point which will have great influence. It is not a new feeding material, but all the evidence points simply to the fact that it has only to become better known and available on a large scale to result in mutual benefits to the farmer, the miller, the manufacturer, and the West African colonies.

COTTON.

The cultivation of fibrous plants, which have made a highly satisfactory start in Togoland and East Africa, are to be found in Cameroon only in the preliminary stage. In the experimental garden, Sanseveria, the Romelia-pita from Central America, manilla hemp, Musa textiles, as well as the Uttari jute, have been planted.

Cotton should have a much greater future than the so-called fibrous plant. It is cultivated at present to a great extent south of Lake Chad by the natives, and the cultivation of cotton has been called systematic, as only one to two year-old plants are harvested. In that region the conditions are so favourable that a considerable development of the cotton cultivation may be counted upon, as soon as more favourable communication conditions are made. In the Benue Valley, cotton has also been cultivated for several decades. The whole of the forest and coastland are unfit for this cultivation, and it is somewhat surprising to hear that on the uncultivated lands of the Mandara Mountains, a very beautiful long fibrous cotton grows. At the instigation of the Colonial Agricultural Committee, cotton cultivation made a tremendous start in Togo, and in East Africa as well as in the Cameroons.

The export of timber has increased by leaps and bounds in recent years. While in 1909 timber to the value of only £8,500 was imported, this sum in 1912 had risen to £35,000, and, with the extension of the railway system, the revenue from this source can be increased almost indefinitely.

EXPERIMENTAL AGRICULTURAL WORK.

Dr. Walter Busse, of the Imperial German Colonial Office, writing in the "Bulletin of the Imperial Institute" on "The Organisation of Experimental Work in Agriculture in the German Colonies," tells us that in Cameroon, as in other parts where land is being opened up for agriculture, the conditions of settlement of the natives, the density of the population, the general standard of civilisation, and the capacity of the natives for any particular kind of activity, all play an important role. "And in proportion as the people incline towards agriculture, so attention must be paid to the inclinations and needs of the separate races, and lastly to the extent, organisation and methods of native agriculture.... The German Colonial Government," the German colonial official proceeds to explain, "has laid it down as a principle that native agriculture in the tropical colonies should be allowed to develop freely side by side with plantations under European control, wherever this does not interfere with higher interests. Local conditions will decide how far in each particular region this or that method of organising agriculture is to be preferred. But wherever climate, soil and condition of settlement do not admit of plantation culture, and a native population capable of production is present, the Government will, as a matter of course, encourage native agriculture as much as possible, and by this means create an improved economic position."

Unfortunately for the native, as Hanns Vischer points out in his article on "Native Education in German Africa," his national feeling, his own industry and aptitude for work, was entirely ignored by the Government, and "higher interests" frequently interfered to retard the development of native enterprise, while the Teutonic professors proved too determined, for the good of colonial agriculture, to transfer to it "the long-approved system of German agriculture, which rests on a strong scientific foundation, built on the results of exact investigation and methods." Germany started her experimental work as soon as she entered upon the occupation of colonies, with the establishment of gardens for raising imported economic plants, such as coffee, cocoa, rubber, &c., in the interest of plantation culture, and for the advancement of gardening and fruit production. When European planters commenced to take up agriculture on their own account, it was found that the experimental work of the botanical gardens was no longer adequate to the new requirements. For this purpose, experimental work on a purely agricultural basis, and an effort to effect an improvement of native agriculture, became necessary. To meet these demands, institutes were established, and agricultural staffs were organised, and the measures taken in Togoland in 1900, for the introduction and extension of cotton cultivation, became the standard for agricultural experimental work in the other tropical African colonies of Cameroon and East Africa.

THE DEPARTMENT OF AGRICULTURE.

The Experimental Institute of Agriculture at Victoria remained as the centre for the whole of the experimental work in Cameroon until the year 1911, when the Imperial Government created a Department of Agriculture at Buea to deal with all questions relating to organisation, while the Victoria Institution continued to undertake the technical and scientific investigations. At first the agricultural work was mainly devoted to assisting the planting industry in the Cameroon Mountains, but as the colony became opened up, fresh problems presented themselves. The reckless exploitation of the *Funtumia elastica* and Landolphia vines in the rubber forests led to the establishment of a special rubber inspectorate, and various arrangements were made for the development of all branches of native cultivation. Special small experimental gardens were created in the larger administrative stations of the interior and placed under the management of a European farmer or gardener, to deal with the cultivation by natives of products suitable for export. Later, a cocoa inspectorate was established to organise native cocoa cultivation in districts in which European cocoa plantations did not and were not likely to exist, and an experimental station was founded in the Jaunde district to encourage the cultivation of such crops as ground-nuts, plantain and manioc, with a view to export. At Kuti and Pittoa two agricultural experimental stations were established, primarily for the cultivation of cotton, but other branches of agriculture, including stock-raising, were embraced in the programme of work at these stations. In 1913 the agricultural staff consisted of fourteen first-grade, seven second-grade and twenty-eight third-grade officers.

The Institute at Victoria comprised a botanic garden and botanical and chemical laboratories, and the work carried on there included the raising of tropical economic plants, experiments in plantation culture and manuring, &c. Since 1910 young natives were trained as plantation managers in the agricultural school attached to the institute. At the cattle-breeding stations at Buea, Dschang and Djuttitsa (in the Dschang district), and Jaunde, the breeding of Allgau bulls and cross-breeding experiments with Allgau bulls and the indigenous humped cows were carried on with the object of obtaining draught cattle for the several districts and supplying meat and dairy produce to the Europeans. At the Dschang School of Agriculture, young natives were instructed in the use of the plough and in other rational methods of agriculture. At the Kuti station, in the Bamum district, and the Pittao station, in the Adamana district, the advancement of cotton cultivation is the primary study, but the programmes of work also include comparative cultivation experiments with indigenous cereals, pulses, root-crops, and fodder plants, the use of the plough, manuring and rotation experiments, cattle-breeding and cattle-keeping, and the training of native travelling instructors.

The Rubber Inspectorate established stations for rubber cultivation at Sangmalima (Ebolowa district), Akonolinga (Jaunde district), Dume (Dume district), and Djahposten (Lomie district), and the work comprised the distribution of Funtumia and Hevea plants to the natives, the superintendence of new plantations, the regeneration of the stocks of wild rubber which had become exhausted by careless exploitation, and the instruction of the natives in the tapping of rubber trees and the preparation and preservation of the rubber.

In order to deal adequately with the agricultural questions which arose locally in the various districts, most of the administrative stations possessed—apart from the established experimental gardens—agricultural officers whose duty it was to superintend local experimental fields and gardens. Such officers were employed, among other places, at Duala, Edea, Bara, Yoko, and Bamenda, the chief aim of the experimental gardens at these places being to develop the cultivation of export products, while experiments with foreign economic plants, yielding produce suitable for export, were also conducted.

MINERAL RESOURCES.

The mining industry has not yet penetrated into the Cameroons, and the mineral deposits of the country are commercially improved. Cretaceous and Tertiary rocks occur in the coastal area and extend northward to the Nigerian border. Gneisses and schists of pre-Cambrian age, with intrusive granites, extend over wide areas in the hinterland, and volcanic rocks of supposed Tertiary age are very abundant. Pegmatites and quartz veins are associated with granite intrusions in the pre-Cambrian rocks. These carry tourmaline in the region north of Duala, as in the Dschang district. Quartz veins with small amounts of pyrite and arsenopyrite also occur.

Tinstone, which occurs in pegmatite veins in Nigeria, may be expected to be encountered in the Cameroons, but although prospecting has been carried on in various parts of the region bordering on Nigeria, in the hope of finding tinstone and wolframite, no results have been obtained. The only trace of gold yet discovered was an occurrence of spangles of gold of theoretical interest only, which was found in a dyke rock (a bostoorite) on the eastern boundary of the Ossidinge district.

Promising finds of mica have been made in the pegmatites of the Ossidinge and Kentu districts, and galena also occurs in the cretaceous sandstone in the Ossidinge district; but hitherto no argentiferous lead-zinc ores comparable with those of Nigeria have been located.

Iron ores, some of which are manganiferous, are abundant in the country. Many of these are of the lateritic type, and furnish material for native smelting, as in other parts of Western Africa. In some localities, iron ore has been formed by the decomposition of basalt. Masses of red and brown ores of this type are found on hill-slopes in the neighbourhood of Bali and Bamenda. A sample of this ore was found to contain 42·25 per cent. of metallic iron, 0·35 of manganese, 0·17 of phosphorus, and 12·26 of silica. Richer ores of the magnetic type are found among the pro-Cambrian gneisses.

Limestones are scarce and of unserviceable quality, but clays and loams, suitable for brick-making, are abundant. Indications of the presence of petroleum in the neighbourhood of Duala were falsified by borings. Asphal is said to occur at Ossidinge and Mamfe on the Cross River. A thin layer of coal yielding 48·3 per cent. of ash has been located at Mamfe. Salt springs exist in the Ossidinge district, and the yield of as much as from 5 to 8 per cent. of sodium-chloride from samples of brine, is believed to indicate that salt beds may be found beneath the surface in this district.

NATIVE EDUCATION

IN order to ascertain the work done by Europeans, the Government and the Missionary Societies in schools for the natives of their various African possessions, the German Colonial Institute in 1911 sent out to the colonies over 2,000 printed *questionnaires*, with a request to the authorities to return answers according to the state of the schools on June 1st in that year. From the information filled in and returned, Herr Missions-Inspector Schlunk, of Hamburg, was able to publish a voluminous report on the subject, and the state of affairs thus revealed is illustrative of the best and worst features of the Teutonic colonising system. The facts in themselves concerning the educational work accomplished in the way of providing the natives with schools and teachers are remarkable.

In Cameroon the first educational work among the natives was begun by the London Baptist Mission in 1845, and in 1885, the year in which the Board of Foreign Missions of the Presbyterian Church in the United States of America entered the field, the London Baptists resigned their organisation to the Missions Gesellschaft, of Basel. Two years later the first Government School was opened in Duala, and in the following four years the Apostolic Vicariat Kamerun, of Limburg on the Lahn, and the German Baptists, of Steglitz, established schools in the colony. In Cameroon, as in Togo, the Government were behind the missions in the number of schools and scholars, having, in 1911, only eight elementary schools, as against the nine of the American Presbyterians, thirty-eight of the German Baptists, eighty-six of the Roman Catholic, and 275 of the Basel Mission. Altogether there were in the colony 499 elementary schools, with forty-two European and 611 native teachers, and 32,056 pupils; twenty-one higher schools, with thirty-three European and thirty native teachers, and 1,802 pupils; eleven industrial schools, with twenty-two European and five native teachers, and 259 pupils; or a total of 531 schools, with ninety-seven European and 646 native teachers, and 34,117 pupils. Of the teachers 3·3 per cent. and of the pupils 8·1 per cent. were females.

THE SCHOOL COURSE.

In both Togo and Cameroon, the course of the elementary schools began with an infant class and lasted four or five years, the objects of the schools in both colonies having been to provide Christian instruction to natives and to train pupils for the higher schools with a view to their entering the service of Europeans. Instruction in German began in the first year, and in the third year pupils were required to read and write German fluently in both characters. The curriculum for the last year included the history of the German Empire since the Franco-German War of 1870-71, the history of the German Emperors since January 18th, 1871, the Geography of Germany, and the singing of German patriotic songs.

In the higher schools, the object of the teachers was to "impart such knowledge as is required in the service of Europeans," and all instruction was given in the German language. The schools for practical work trained girls for domestic work, laundry work and farming, while boys received instruction in carpentering, cabinet-making, smiths' work, boot-making and tailoring, printing and book-binding. At the completion of their course, all pupils were obliged to remain in the service of the Government for two or more years. In both Togoland and Cameroon, the Government had a school of agriculture, where pupils were instructed in farming, especially cotton-growing and the use of the plough, and at some of the mission schools in the latter colony the pupils were trained in brick-making and cocoa-planting, and the work connected with water-supply and bridge-making.

In both colonies the schools generally were open on five or six days a week, with from twenty to thirty-five hours' instruction per week, according to the grade of the several schools. The average length of holidays for Mission and Government schools was from two to three months per annum. Unfortunately, no statement of revenue or expenditure is included in the case of Togoland beyond the fact that the Government made a yearly grant of £750, distributed among the various schools for the encouragement of German language-study. In Cameroon, in 1910, the Basel Mission spent £5,386 on teachers' salaries, and the Roman Catholics £1,626. The cost of the Government schools in that year was £1,963. Generally no school fees were paid except in some of the higher schools in Togo, where pupils paid 50s. per annum, and at Garna, in Cameroon, the Government pupils paid 30s. per annum in kind.

THE RESULTS OF GERMAN METHODS.

In Cameroon a Government Proclamation of April 25th, 1910, made school attendance obligatory for all native children, instruction in German from the first class was made law, and the punishment for a child who left school before completing the whole course was fixed at a fine of £2 10s. or a flogging. Although children generally were anxious to attend school in order to qualify for service with Europeans, truantry appears to have become more popular after obligatory attendance was introduced, and the native police were kept busy in bringing back absentees. School children, who were distinguished by the wearing of brass-buttons and cockades, showed a tendency to become denationalised: few of them returned to the family farms when they completed their school course, which had the effect of causing them to lose touch with their own tribe and families.

It is impossible, after reading Herr Missions-Inspector Schlunk's report, to refuse admiration to the thoroughness of the German system of instituting these inquiries, or to the care with which the Germans lay themselves out to Teutonise their native subjects. Their organising ability, as revealed in their methods of imparting instruction to the natives and preparing their minds for the reception of *kultur*, is amazing, but as Hanns Vischer shows in his analysis of this informative publication, contributed to the *Journal of the African Society*, their method has its disadvantages. "Little love and scarcely any respect for the native," he comments, "are to be found among the various reports. No mention is ever made of the natives' national feeling. Natives are taught German history and the names of the German Emperors, and they can sing German patriotic songs. From every colony we hear that the boys who have been to school seldom or never return to their own surroundings, and although this is regretted, as being detrimental to the interests of a peasant community, no mention is made of the breaking-up of the native family and the inevitable harm which must follow. The importance of practical instruction is everywhere recommended to teach the native to work, but no mention is made of the natives' own industry and love for work which might be developed."

THE CAMEROON-NIGERIAN BOUNDARY

THE country bordering on the Nigerian boundary from Yola to Obokum on the Cross River, a distance of 360 miles, and the peoples inhabiting the several districts it passes through, have been admirably dealt with by Captain W. V. Nugent, R.A. Captain Nugent, who had been a member of the Commission under Colonel Whitlock which surveyed this area between 1907 and 1909, was sent out in August, 1912, to mark the boundary between the Cameroon and the Nigerias along the line which had been previously settled approximately on the map at a conference between the British and German Governments. The British Commissioner and his assistants met Lieut. Detzner, the German Commissioner, on October 8th, 1912, and the work of demarcation continued without interruption for six months, during which time 116 pillars were placed in position. Both Commissioners wrote accounts of this Anglo-German Frontier Demarcation Expedition, but, while Lieut. Detzner's official article on the subject, published in *Deutsches Kolonialblatt* (1913) is a dull, pedantic and unsatisfactory document, the paper read by Captain Nugent before the Royal Geographical Society in March, 1914, is compact of information and extremely interesting, and it is from his descriptions that I have derived the following details and extracts.

The frontier line divides the mountains, torrential streams

and sparsely-inhabited areas of the Cameroons form the wide fertile plains, great navigable waterways and densely populated districts on the Nigerian side of the border. The fact that Benue River and its three great southern tributaries, the Teraba, Donga and Katsena Rivers, all rise on the plateaux of the Central Cameroon, and only become navigable for canoes upon entering Nigerian territory, explain the unequal distribution of man over the country; for, while the savage pagan tribes have withdrawn to the almost inaccessible hilltops, the more civilised agricultural and trading peoples have kept to the well-watered plains.

THE FULANI REGION.

The boundary line, which commences at Byaaer, a three days' march from Yola, crosses the M'Bulo plain and follows the Upper M'Bulo river to its source in the Shebshi Mountains. "The plain," to quote from Captain Nugent's description, "is covered with thin bush, and dotted with villages, each with its surrounding patches of cultivation. The formation is brown laterite, the rocks containing occasional bands and lumps of ironstone." The lower slopes of the isolated granite hills, which rise above the general level, are covered with pagan villages. "The people inhabiting the plains on both sides of the boundary are Fulanis, subject to the Emirs of Yola and Nassarawa; but the tops of isolated mountains, and the narrow valleys between the long spurs jutting out from the Shebshi group, are inhabited by pagans, offshoots of the Chamba and Dakka tribes. The habits and customs of the Fulanis are well known—they are by nature herdsmen, just as the Hausas are born traders and the pagans agriculturists. The country is rich in flocks and herds of cattle, sheep and goats. A large trade is also done in horses. The villages consist of round huts of sun-baked mud, with conical roofs thatched with dry grass. Sometimes, when the village is only intended to be temporary, the walls of the huts are made of zana matting, which is also used to enclose the compounds, or groups of huts inhabited by one family. Every village has its assembly place, generally under a large shady tree, where the headman and his advisers sit all day and smoke, while the slaves work in the fields or drive the cattle to pasture. Slave-dealing is still carried on in this country, advantage being taken of the proximity of the boundary, which makes it so easy to evade justice.... The work of marking the boundary was watched with the greatest interest by the Fulani population. The 'kings' of all the towns on the English side, and a good many from the German side, came to salute us, generally bringing a present of a fowl or a basket of limes. Each 'king' carries a long stick, surmounted by a brass crown, the emblem of his office under the Government. There are first, second and third class 'kings'; the size of the crown varies accordingly."

The line in crossing the Shebshi Mountains passes over the summit of Mount Dakka, upon which the boundary pillar is 5,388 feet above sea level. "The view from Dakka is magnif-icent. On all sides are tumbled masses of mountain, much cut up by deep ravines and rocky gorges, through which the many headwaters of the M'Bulo and Kam rivers tear headlong to the plains. On the German side, Vogel Spitz rises amid innumerable peaks and valleys to a height of nearly 7,000 feet, overlooking some hundred square miles of still unknown country. The northern spurs, projecting into the Cameroons, enclose high table-lands, extraordinarily fertile and highly cultivated.... The boundary crosses the plateau near the only practicable pass, the road being entirely on the German side, so that one result of the demarcation is to close the direct trade route between M'Bulo and Kam Valleys until a new pass is discovered. There are plenty of tracks over these mountains, but very few practicable for animals. A bull which costs £1 at Tibak, in the M'Bulo Valley, is worth £3 or £4 at Gankita, in the Kam Valley, the distance as the crow flies between these two places being no more than twelve miles."

THE SHEBSHI MOUNTAINEERS.

"The Shebshi Mountains are interesting from the fact that they would form the principal obstacle, a well-nigh insuperable one, to the construction of a direct line of railway from Calabar, or a point on the Cross River, *via* Takum and Bakundi, to Yola. Yola is one of the few important points in Nigeria which does not appear likely to be linked up with the coast by a railway for many years to come. The German railway from Duala to the north, if it ever does reach Garua, will pass to the east of the Shebshis, where many obstacles, almost as formidable, will have to be overcome....

"The people inhabiting the Shebshi Mountains and their foothills are principally Chamba and Dakka pagans. They have many points in common with other hill pagans of Northern Nigeria and Adamawa. The effect of Mohammedan inroads upon these tribes is especially evident. They may be divided into two classes: firstly, those who are slaves and mingle freely with the Fulanis, their villages being in the plain; and, secondly, those who hold themselves aloof on the hill-tops. The former have copied many things from the Fulanis, such as clothing, houses, &c.—almost everything, in fact, except their pastoral proclivities. The pagan will keep goats and fowls, but he will have nothing to do with horses and cattle.

"It is with the hill-top pagans, however, that we are principally concerned, as nine-tenths of the whole boundary zone are inhabited by people of this denomination. The first sign of the lower stage of civilization is the absence of clothing. A tuft of grass is the national dress, and even this is often dispensed with.

"The villages consist of little beehive-shaped huts of mud or grass, perched on apparently inaccessible heights, or cunningly hidden away in mazes of dense tropical vegetation. The inhabitants bear a great resemblance to monkeys, being small in stature, but extraordinarily active. The steepest and most difficult ascent over rocks and ravines is to them as easy as a straight, broad, level road. In fact, I have often noticed that these pagans, made to carry a load on the level, are utterly at a loss. They only come down from their rocky fastnesses to cultivate their fields, or to make war on their neighbours. They are armed with bows and poisoned arrows, from which it is never safe for them to be parted, even when working in the fields. They are almost invariably at war with a neighbouring village, the probable reason being that some of their women have been carried off. No regular trade is indulged in, but they are very fond of salt, which they obtain from Hausa traders. A bag of salt which costs half-a-crown on the coast has a purchasing power of at least ten shillings in this country.

"Each village is an independent community under a chief. The inhabitants are entirely ignorant of the world beyond the next village to their own. The nominal chief of the village has not, as a rule, as much influence as the local ju-ju man or witch doctor, whose power over these extremely superstitious people is directly proportionate to his success in imposing upon their credulity. Any calamity, such as an epidemic of sickness or a sudden death, is always attributed to the evil eye, and some member of the community is at once suspected, and either killed or sold to passing Hausa traders. If a chief dies, the village always moves to another site. This partly accounts for the number of deserted villages and ruins found in the Shebshi Mountains.

"The Chambas are industrious agriculturists, and keep large numbers of goats and fowls in their villages. The farms are generally at the foot of the hills. After the harvest the people brew large supplies of spirit from the grain, and get drunk for several days together. These orgies generally result in fighting among themselves. The principal industry, besides agriculture, is working in iron. They make their own farm implements, spear and arrow heads, and pipe-stems."

THE TERABA VALLEY.

From Dakka the boundary line follows the Kam for about a dozen miles, and then, leaving the river, it runs over a block of hills which form the fringe of a vast unknown tract of the Cameroon country. Here the hill-top villages are few, the inhabitants are wilder and more squalid than the Dakka natives, and the land is the haunt of the elephant, the lion, the bush-cow and the leopard. From these hills the boundary descends into the valley of the River Lumen, which runs for twenty or thirty miles under a dark arch of overhanging trees. The water of the Lumen is very cold, even in the heat of the day, and the sands of the river are full of iron. The line crosses the Lumen and mounts a high ridge, called Shina, to descend again into the vast plain of the River Teraba.

Along the banks of the Teraba are numerous Hausa and Jukum villages, situated on important trade roads between Northern Nigeria and Cameroon, the principal trade being in rubber, kola nuts, sheep, and goats. There are no cattle, as many kinds of biting fly, including the tsetse, have their breeding places in this area. As the Teraba is typical of all the great southern tributaries of the Benue, the following short description, which Captain Nugent gives of one of the upper reaches, will be read with interest:—

"Fifteen miles above Karbabi the river bends sharply at right angles, forming noisy rapids. Above the rapids the bed is rocky with deep pools. Under the tall trees along the banks are open glades like an English beech wood, entirely free from under-growth, the ground being carpeted with soft moss. There are the feeding-grounds of huge herds of hippopotami, who live in the pools in the daytime. The river is here 200 to 300 yards wide, with high banks; the channel winds among huge boulders, forming a chain of pools, but leaving a narrow deep waterway among the larger rocks. The pools are like dark mirrors, silent and stagnant, yet bright and clear, reflecting the trees on the opposite bank in full detail. Wild geese and ibis fly overhead, whilst large alligators move about like torpedoes, with their noses out of the water, leaving long trails of bubbles on the surface.

"There is no village within many miles of this place, and it was only with the greatest difficulty that we could obtain guides, as there are no tracks except those made by the larger game. The inhabitants of the pools were thoroughly startled at our approach. There seemed to be a sort of collusion between the different birds and beasts. The shrieking ibis warned the alligators asleep on the rocks in the sun, they, in alarm, slid into the water and warned the river-horse that something was amiss; the river-horse in his turn went pounding up-stream, under water, coming up to breathe at intervals behind the rocks and branches. The snorting was terrific. We estimated that there were between thirty and forty hippopotami in the largest pool. I have never seen a wilder-looking place; it seemed to be alive with everything except humanity.

IN THE CANNIBAL COUNTRY.

"The boundary after crossing the Gazuba River, a tributary of the Teraba, again ascends into an unexplored continuation of the Banjo highlands, and drops into the plain of the Donga Valley. The inhabitants here are a mixture of Jukums and Zumperis, but there are numerous settlements of Hausas, whose trade consists of smuggling rubber and kola nuts into Nigeria without paying the German tax. The pagans, who live in 'swallow-nest' villages on the heights, cultivate guinea-corn and root crops, while yams, cassava and sweet potatoes grow in abundance in the interstices between the huts. The boundary reaches the Donga, and after following the river for fifteen miles and crossing the plateau of the Wanya Mountains, reaches the plain of the Bamana Valley, in which oil palms are first encountered.

"The country between the Gamana and Katsena Rivers is inhabited by Zumperi pagans, who are cannibals and live on hill-tops. They are of small stature and of remarkably repulsive appearance. Every other man appeared to be suffering from goitre or elephantiasis—whether the legacy of cannibalism, or the effect of drinking infected water, it is difficult to say. The people are industrious, and besides corn, grow large quantities of cotton and tobacco on the hillsides. They breed dogs for eating purposes, and all the villages are full of yelping curs, covered with sores like their owners. In one village a large deposit of human skulls was seen. The villages are well built and surrounded by mud walls and ditches. Among the numerous 'ju-jus' found in the deserted huts was a grotesque mask, which was apparently kept to frighten the women. Any woman seeing it must die at once. When the community is short of meat, the local witch doctor puts on the mask and runs about the hills until he meets a likely looking victim, who is then killed and eaten. The Zumperis are great hunters, and have killed off nearly all the game in their country except leopards."

MUNCHI CIVILISATION.

From the Zumperi country the Commission traversed the undulating plain that connects it with the valley of the Katsena, the last of the three great tributaries of the Benue, and ascending this valley reached the Agara or Misa Munchis district. The branch of the large and powerful Munchi tribe which inhabits this area have preserved themselves from contamination with the neighbouring tribes, by whom they are greatly feared. The Munchis of the plains, who are of good physique and very intelligent, are supposed to have come originally from a country called Para, somewhere north of Yola, and they still call themselves Para among themselves. Many of their customs are similar to the Zulus, with whom they have often been compared, and the majority of their laws are identical with those of Leviticus. Their villages are well built and clean, and the men are brave in war and industrious in peace. Their marriage customs, in addition to the payment of a dowry, include exchanges of sisters, daughters and sometimes wives. Polygamy is rife, and the value of a dowry varies from two cows in the case of a young girl, to one cow or less in the case of a widow or elderly woman.

"The Munchis are of striking appearance. Those near the boundary are poor and wear few clothes. They go in for extravagant hairdressing, the most popular coiffure being a shaven head with one or two balls of hair left growing. Others wear their hair in beaded strands, falling over the side of the face. The tribal markings are a number of raised tattoo marks, in the form of a crescent, on both sides of the temple. These are universal, and are compulsory for both sexes, but the marks disappear in old age. Other markings are tattoed stars and rings on the forehead, chest and back, but these are all optional. The two front teeth of the upper jaw are filed into V-shape.

"The Munchis are excellent farmers, and grow guinea-corn, yams, millet, beniseed, maize, and ground-nuts in large quantities. They also cultivate cotton, from which they weave good cloth, dyeing is with indigo, which is grown round every compound. Each village has at least one public dye-pit. Tobacco is also grown, and is either used as snuff or smoked in large pipes with bowls of clay and stems of smelted brass.

"They are clever workers in wood and iron, making chairs and stools, in the carving of which they display some art and much ingenuity. The iron ore found locally used to be smelted in large quantities, and the remains of old workings can be seen in many places, but trade iron bars are now more generally used: from these spears and arrow-heads, hoes, knives, and daggers are constructed. The small knives are curious in shape, the handles being iron loops, which fit over the palm of the hand. The hoes have broad, heavy blades, fitted with short, crooked wooded handles, and are most effective agricultural implements. The principal weapons of offence are bows and arrows, the arrows being poisoned with a compound of crushed and boiled strophanthus seeds, snakes' heads, and poisonous plants, &c., which when freshly made is very potent, the slightest scratch causing a man to die in agony in twenty minutes. The fumes from this poison, when it is being boiled, are very deadly, even in the open air. The mixing is always done by one of the numerous ju-ju men, who profess to have antidotes, both external and internal, but there is no authenticated case of a cure having been seen by any European up to date.

"In every village there is a large war-drum, constructed from a hollowed-out log, over which is stretched a hide. The Munchis are expert in the use of these drums for signalling purposes, and messages are sent in code from village to village throughout their country with great rapidity and accuracy.

"They are very fond of dances and plays, which, accompanied by songs, are held on the occasion of the death of a chief or the headman of a compound, also at births and marriages. These dances are often kept up for several days when the host is rich enough to supply the food and drink, the latter being an intoxicating liquid distilled from guinea-corn.

THE GRASS LAND REGION.

"Leaving the Munchis' country, the Commission came to the junction of the Amiri and Mahana Rivers—whose steep banks are lined with magnificent trees, from which hang long ribbon orchids over a series of deep clear pools full of large fish—in a region of open grass land. The road up the Amiri Valley passes through extensive yam fields and Olitti and Atcho' villages, composed of roomy, massive houses in small stone-walled compounds, protected with loop-holed thorn palisades. Grass land is reached at a height of 4,000 feet, and the path after crossing five separate peaks of 2,000 feet reaches the main ridge about 5,000 feet above sea level. To the north and east, as far as the eye can see, stretches open grass land, with range upon range of blue mountains in the distance. Across the plain sweep parallel shining rivers, disappearing through gaps in the hills to the north. To the south and west, the great forest-clad plain extends to the Cross River, whose valley forty miles away is marked by a long bank of clouds. All around is high tableland, cut up into small plateaux by numerous ravines, down which countless streams tear headlong to the plains."

Descending from the main plateau, which is covered with thick short grass and appears to be an ideal district for cattle raising, the Commission came to the first villages of the Anyangs, who are almost invariably at war with the grass land people. "Their villages are hidden away in the forest, and consist of long, low, rectangular mud houses with roofs of palm-leaves, on either side of a squalid street. The people are very poor, and live almost entirely on plantains, their farms being in small clearings, widely separated. Pigs are kept in large numbers in the villages. Further south, the people met with are Bokis, who extend to the Cross River.... The village boundaries, although in dense forest, are well known to the natives, who are extremely jealous of their rubber-collecting rights."

The geological structure of the boundary zone, taken as a whole, is said to present few features of interest. Traces of tin were found in some of the rivers flowing north from the watershed of the Cross River and Benue system, and nearly all the rivers crossed by the Commission contained traces of monazite. The occasional belts of forest along the streams in the open bush country, north of the watershed between the Benue and Cross River systems, are mostly full of vine rubber (*Landolphia*). The forest line to the south of the Benue-Cross River watershed extends without a break to the Cross River, and from there to the sea. The trees grow to a great height, and the whole forest abounds in ebony, mahogany and other valuable timbers. The rains in the boundary districts begin in March with a few violent tornadoes, which become more frequent and less violent until May, and from that month till September heavy rain falls almost every day. By the end of September the rivers are in full flood, and the low-lying country is under water. In October the steady rain ceases, and at the end of the month the dry season sets in.

NEW CAMEROON.

The region of New Cameroon which was added to the German territory under the Franco-German Agreement of November 4th, 1911, was represented as being swampy, depopulated, and devastated by sleeping sickness, and the Teuton acquisition was greeted with general derision. But a more thorough investigation of the possession has shown that it is not so bad as it was painted, and while there are tracts that hold out no promises of profitable development, there are districts in the New Cameroon which will handsomely repay exploitation. The German "frontier" expedition into the interior has published descriptions of a steppe region covered with tall grasses, bushes, and trees interspersed with grassy plains. The country abounds with a variety of animals, including giraffes, antelopes, gazelles, buffaloes, zebras, rhinoceri, elephants, and apes, and the Lagone and its tributaries contain large quantities of fish. It is inhabited by the Lakka tribe, a very independent race of Sudan negroes, who live in villages and disclose many differences in languages, manners, and customs. Hunting and fishing are their secondary occupation, but their regular occupation is agriculture. Their well-tilled fields, fertilised with the ashes of burnt grass, produce millet, ground-nuts, tobacco, hemp, and cotton, and their greatest delicacies are dried fish and caterpillars. They possess a few horses and goats, and the women employ themselves in pottery and basket work when not engaged in agriculture. Herr Eltester says that the Pangwe tribe, inhabiting the Muni district, are distinguished by every conceivable bad quality. They are thieves, liars, and idlers, and are given to indolence. The men sit around in the villages and smoke, the boys lay traps for wild animals, and the women till the fields.

THE DIFFICULTIES OF DEVELOPMENT.

The greatest drawback to the systematic development of the Cameroons is the naturally bad means of communication as regards both roads and waterways. The country being largely of steppe-like formation, the rivers are frequently interrupted by rapids and waterfalls. The chief rivers, the Munga, Wuri, and Sanaga, are only navigable by steamers for a distance of seventy kilometres. Beyond this point, litter-transport has to be employed, and as bearers can only carry loads of 60 to 70 lbs. for a distance of from twenty to twenty-five kilometres a day, and as the distance from Duala, the coast station, to Central Cameroon is a thirty days' journey, and to Lake Chad twenty days', few products, except ivory and rubber, can bear this expensive means of transport. The most important tasks before the Government which is entrusted with the future of the Cameroons is the amplification of the means of communication, the encouragement of native civilisation, the exploitation of the economic resources of the valuable hinterland, and the extension of the plantation system. The enormous physical difficulties in the way of railway construction must not be under-estimated. The country is covered with colossal tropical growths, which must be cleared, the plague of sleeping-sickness must be stamped out, and the dreaded tsetse fly banished. In such regions railway building is arduous and costly, but not until the rich regions hitherto unreached have been brought into communication with the coast, will the Cameroons begin to profit by its "unlimited possibilities."

COLOURED PLATE

PLATE 1

DUALA.

PLATE 2

THE QUAY AT DUALA.

PLATE 3

LANDING-PLACE AT DUALA.

PLATE 4

POST OFFICE, DUALA.

PLATE 5

COURT HOUSE AT DUALA.

PLATE 6

HOSPITAL AT DUALA.

NATIVES' METAL WORK.

PLATE 8

THE BÂLE MISSION AT DUALA.

WORKSHOP OF THE BÂLE MISSION, DUALA.

PLATE 10

MANGA BELI'S PALACE, DUALA.

THE NATIVE QUARTER, DUALA.

BUSINESS OFFICES IN DUALA.

PLATE 13

NATIVES WOOD CARVING.

PLATE 14

THE WOERMANN FLOATING DOCK AT DUALA.

PLATE 15

LANDING JETTY.

PLATE 16

CONSTRUCTING THE CENTRAL RAILWAY FROM DUALA TO THE
NYONG RIVER.

VIEW OF THE WURI RIVER AT BONABERI.

THE WURI RIVER ABOVE DUALA.

PLATE 19

ELEPHANT GRASS.

PLATE 20

BUEA, FORMER SEAT OF THE GERMAN GOVERNMENT
OF CAMEROON. GREAT CAMEROON MOUNTAINS IN THE
BACKGROUND.

PLATE 21

VIEW OF BUEA.

PLATE 22

THE LATE GERMAN GOVERNOR'S PALACE, BUEA.

BUEA.

ALGAU CATTLE GRAZING NEAR BUEA.

GRAZING LAND NEAR BUEA.

PLATE 26

TOBACCO PLANTATION NEAR BUEA.

PLATE 27

THE NEW OKOTI CRATER ON THE CAMEROON MOUNTAIN
TAKEN FROM THE EAST.

PLATE 28

FOREST ON THE CAMEROON PEAK, AT AN ELEVATION OF 1,800
METRES.

VIEW OF VICTORIA.

VICTORIA, WITH THE GREAT CAMEROON MOUNTAIN AND
LITTLE CAMEROON MOUNTAIN.

PLATE 31

VIEW OF AMBAS BAY.

PLATE 32

STEEP COAST NEAR VICTORIA.

PLATE 33

BOTANICAL GARDENS, VICTORIA.

PLATE 34

OFFICE IN THE BOTANICAL GARDENS, VICTORIA.

PLATE 35

BUILDINGS OF THE VICTORIA CO., VICTORIA.

PLATE 36

VEGETATION IN THE FOREST.

PLATE 37

KRIBI, AT THE MOUTH OF THE KRIBI RIVER, THE CHIEF
TRADING-PLACE ON THE COAST OF SOUTH CAMEROON.

PLATE 38

KRIBI.

PLATE 39

LOW-LYING COAST NEAR KRIBI.

PLATE 40

MISSION HOUSE AT KRIBI.

PLATE 41

BOA-CONSTRICTOR.

PLATE 42

NATIVES OF BULE.

MARSHY LAND IN THE OIL-PALM REGION NEAR THE COAST.

PLATE 44

OIL-PALM IN A MAIZE FIELD.

PLATE 45

PREPARATION OF PALM-OIL BY NATIVE METHODS.

PLATE 46

OIL-PALMS.

PLATE 47

COCOA TREE WITH FRUIT.

PLATE 48

SEVEN-YEAR-OLD OIL-PALM TREES.

THE OIL-PALM. CROWN WITH CLUSTERS OF FRUIT.

PLATE 50

STATION YARD AT EDEA.

PLATE 51

THE SANAGA RIVER NEAR EDEA.

PLATE 52

THE SANAGA RIVER NEAR EDEA.

PLATE 53

BRIDGE OVER THE SOUTHERN ARM OF THE SANAGA RIVER
(DUALA-NYONG RAILWAY).

PLATE 54

ENTRANCE TO THE FOREST NEAR EDEA.

PLATE 55

WOERMANN LINE BOATS ON THE SANAGA RIVER.

PLATE 56

RAPIDS IN THE SANAGA RIVER.

MAIZE STORES AT JAUNDE.

PARK-LIKE DISTRICT IN A CLEARING OF THE FOREST ON THE
EDEA-JAUNDE ROAD.

PLATE 59

NATIVE SOLDIERS AT JAUNDE.

PLATE 60

NATIVE TROOPS IN CAMP.

NATIVE TROOPS ON ACTIVE SERVICE.

PLATE 62

NATIVE VILLAGE. GABLED HUTS.

PLATE 63

ON THE UPPER NYONG RIVER.

PLATE 64

COLONIAL TROOPS AT A FACTORY ON THE UPPER NYONG
RIVER.

PLATE 65

FERRY BOAT ON THE NYONG RIVER.

PLATE 66

STEAMER AT THE LANDING-PLACE OF A FACTORY ON THE
NYONG RIVER.

COLLECTING RUBBER IN THE FOREST.

DEHANE RUBBER PLANTATION (NYONG RIVER).

PLATE 69

DEHANE RUBBER PLANTATION (NYONG RIVER).

PLATE 70

MANAGER'S HOUSE ON THE DEHANE RUBBER PLANTATION.

CLEARING THE GROUND FOR PLANTING RUBBER TREES.

PLATE 72

GROUND CLEARED FOR PLANTING.

MIXED TREES IN A PLANTATION.

PLATE 74

PAY DAY ON A RUBBER PLANTATION.

A PATH THROUGH THE DEHANE PLANTATION ON THE NYONG
RIVER.

PLATE 76

NATIVES WAITING FOR THE DINNER BELL.

BANANA TREES ON A RUBBER PLANTATION.

PLATE 78

A FOUR-YEAR-OLD RUBBER TREE READY FOR TAPPING.

NATIVES AT DEHANE.

ROLL CALL OF LABOURERS ON A PLANTATION.

ELEPHANT GRASS.

TAPPING THE RUBBER TREE.

PLATE 83

SMALL HUTS FOR PATIENTS SUFFERING FROM SLEEPING
SICKNESS.

PLATE 84

FOREST ON THE BANKS OF THE MUNGO RIVER.

PLATE 85

NATIVE SUSPENSION BRIDGE OVER THE MUNGO RIVER.

PLATE 86

NATIVE SUSPENSION BRIDGE OVER THE MUNGO RIVER.

THE "MUNGO" GERMAN GOVERNMENT STEAMER ON THE RIVER.

PLATE 88

A TREE TRUNK USED AS A BRIDGE.

VILLAGE OF NINONG AT THE WESTERN BASE OF THE
MANENGUBA MOUNTAINS.

PLATE 90

THE ELONG MOUNTAIN IN THE BAMENDA RANGE SEEN FROM
THE FOOT OF THE MANENGUBA MOUNTAINS.

FOREST ON THE BANKS OF THE CROSS RIVER.

PLATE 92

FISHING ON THE CROSS RIVER.

PLATE 93

THE CROSS RIVER AT NSSANAKANG.

PLATE 94

FACTORY ON THE CROSS RIVER FOR TRADING WITH THE
NATIVES.

BANANA TREES NEAR OSSIDINGE.

PLATE 96

A VILLAGE IN KEAKALAND, OSSIDINGE.

PLATE 97

HEAD-DRESS AND TRIBAL MARKS OF KEAKA WOMEN.

PLATE 98

NATIVE MUSICAL INSTRUMENTS IN KEAKALAND.

PLATE 99

CARAVAN CROSSING THE NDI RIVER, NEAR FONTSCHANDA.

PLATE 100

TYPICAL VEGETATION.

A PALM GROVE.

A SUSPENSION BRIDGE.

PLATE 103

A SUSPENSION BRIDGE.

PLATE 104

SUSPENSION BRIDGE OVER THE FI, NEAR TINTO.

FUMBAN IN BAMUM.

PLATE 106

NATIVE MARKET AT BAMUM. PROVISIONS AND KOLO NUTS
BEING SOLD.

NDJOIA, SULTAN OF BAMUM, BETWEEN TWO WAR DRUMS, AT
FUMBAN.

PLATE 108

SULTAN OF BAMUM WITH THE CAPTAINS OF HIS TROOPS.

MADE BY THE NATIVES OF BAMUM.

PLATE 110

TRIAL FIELD FOR COTTON AND TOBACCO AT THE
GOVERNMENT STATION, FUMBAN, BAMUM.

PLATE 111

BAMUM. NOTE THE FRIEZE OF ANIMALS UNDER THE GRASS
ROOF.

PLATE 112

STREET SCENE IN BAMUM.

STREET SCENE IN BAMUM.

PLATE 114

STREET SCENE IN BAMUM.

PLATE 115

A HOUSE IN BAMUM.

PLATE 116

A STREET IN THE WOMEN'S QUARTER.

COTTON FIELD NEAR BAMUM.

PLATE 118

DRACÆNA, THE FETISH TREES OF WEST AFRICA.

MARKET-PLACE AT BANJO, WITH THE BANJO MOUNTAINS IN
THE DISTANCE.

PLATE 120

THE "MALAM" OF BANJO IN HAUSA STATE COSTUME.

BANJO, A SETTLEMENT IN THE INTERIOR.

PLATE 122

VEGETATION IN THE FOREST.

PLATE 123

THE "ISLAND" MOUNTAIN DISTRICT IN NORTH ADAMAUA BETWEEN NTEM AND THE RIBÄU SLOPE ON THE BANJO ROAD.

PLATE 124

GRANITE MOUNTAIN IN CENTRAL CAMEROON.

SUDAN NATIVES OF CENTRAL CAMEROON. WUTE NATIVES IN WAR COSTUME.

PLATE 126

WAR GAMES OF THE WUTE NATIVES.

WOMAN OF THE WUTE TRIBE.

PLATE 128

WOMAN OF THE WUTE TRIBE.

SUDAN NATIVES IN CENTRAL CAMEROON. WUTE ARCHERS.

PLATE 130

SUDAN NATIVES IN CENTRAL CAMEROON. WUTES WITH THEIR
WAR DRUMS.

PLATE 131

HUMP-BACKED CATTLE OF ADAMAUA.

PLATE 132

HUMP-BACKED CATTLE OF ADAMAUA.

PLATE 133

THE FARO ABOVE TSCHAMBA.

PLATE 134

CARAVAN TRAVELLING—RESTING.

PLATE 135

KUMBO HIGHLANDS ON THE WAY TO LAKE MAUWE, BETWEEN
BAKUMBI AND BANKA.

PLATE 136

KUMBO HIGHLANDS BETWEEN BANKA AND LAKE MAUWE.

PLATE 137

THE REMAINS OF A VOLCANO IN THE KUMBO HIGHLANDS.

PLATE 138

FOREST IN THE HIGHLANDS.

CHANGE FROM FOREST TO GRASS COUNTRY ON THE BROKEN
EDGE OF THE INNER HIGHLANDS NEAR FONTEM.

PLATE 140

CULTIVATED PORTIONS OF GRASS COUNTRY.

PLATE 141

TYPICAL GRASS COUNTRY IN BAFU-FONDONG, ON THE GREAT
DSCHANG-BAMENDA ROAD.

PLATE 142

WOMEN WORKING IN THE FIELDS IN THE GRASS COUNTRY,
NORTH-WEST CAMEROON.

DEATH DANCE OF THE NATIVES NEAR DSCHANG.

PLATE 144

THE CHIEF BAFU-FONDONG ON HIS THRONE.

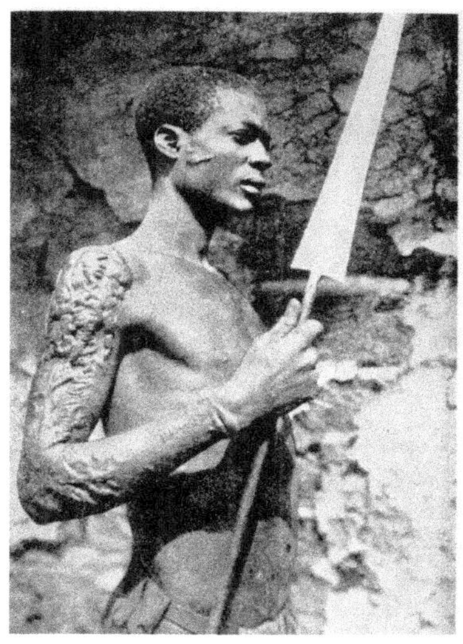

TATOOED FONDONG NEGRO.

A CHIEF'S WIFE IN THE GRASS COUNTRY.

PLATE 147

PARASITES ON A TREE, NEAR THE GRASS COUNTRY.

PLATE 148

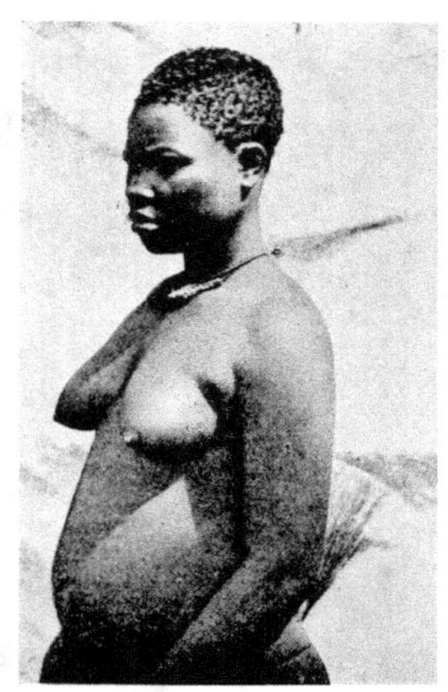

BALI NEGRESS IN THE GRASS COUNTRY.

PLATE 149

MBO, A FORTIFIED STATION NEAR THE GRASS COUNTRY.

PLATE 150

KUSSERI, A FORTIFIED STATION IN NORTH CAMEROON.

THE RESIDENT'S HOUSE AT KUSSERI.

MECCA PILGRIMS AT KUSSERI.

LOG PATH THROUGH A SWAMP.

PLATE 154

HORSEMEN IN NORTH CAMEROON.

PLATE 155

VIEW OF ELEPHANT LAKE.

PLATE 156

VILLAGE OF KILGRIM IN THE MANDARA MOUNTAINS.

PLATE 157

THE LAGONE RIVER AT MUSGUM.

PLATE 158

CARAVAN CROSSING A RIVER.

PLATE 159

NJOJA, WITH HIS WIVES AND CHILDREN, SITTING IN FRONT OF
HIS PALACE.

PLATE 160

BAKWIRI WOMEN AND CHILDREN DANCING.

THE HEAD CHIEF BALWEN IN HIS WAR COSTUME.

PLATE 162

CHIEFTAIN IN GALA ATTIRE.

HAUSA GIRL AT A SPRING.

PLATE 164

NATIVES OF NORTH CAMEROON.
1. The "Lamido" of Banjo (Fullah).

2. Hausa Traders.

3. Arab from Lake Chad.

PLATE 165

DENG-DENG, A SETTLEMENT IN THE INTERIOR.

PLATE 166

DIKOA, A SETTLEMENT IN THE INTERIOR.

PLATE 167

EBOLOWA, A SETTLEMENT IN THE INTERIOR.

PLATE 168

FLOODS NEAR SSIGAL.

SULTAN OF NGAUMDERE WITH HIS BODYGUARD.

PLATE 170

MARKET AT NGAUMDERE.

MAIN BUILDINGS OF THE BIBUNDI PLANTATION.

PLATE 172

BUNGALOW ON THE BIBUNDI PLANTATION.

PLATE 173

PLANTATION IN FULL BEARING.

PLATE 174

BAIA YOUTHS.

BAIA WOMEN.

PLATE 176

DEAD ELEPHANT.

WALRUS.

A HAUSA VILLAGE.

A NATIVE VILLAGE. MUSGUM HUTS.

PLATE 180

A NATIVE VILLAGE. HUTS WITH CONE-SHAPED ROOFS.

PLATE 181

CARAVAN TRAVELLING. HIRING CARRIERS.

PLATE 182

RUBBER CARAVAN.

IVORY CARAVAN.

SCENE AT AN IVORY FACTORY.

WEIGHING THE IVORY.

FACTORY IN THE INTERIOR OF SOUTH CAMEROON.

ROLL-CALL OF LABOURERS.

BRIDGING OVER A RAVINE.

PLATE 189

SAWING WOOD.

PLATE 190

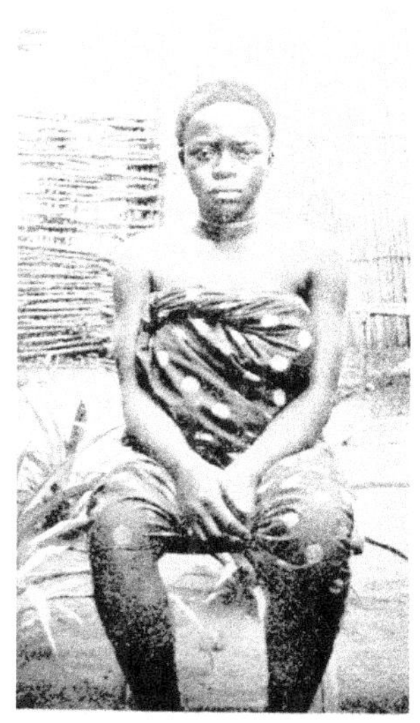

NJEM WOMAN, SOUTH CAMEROON.

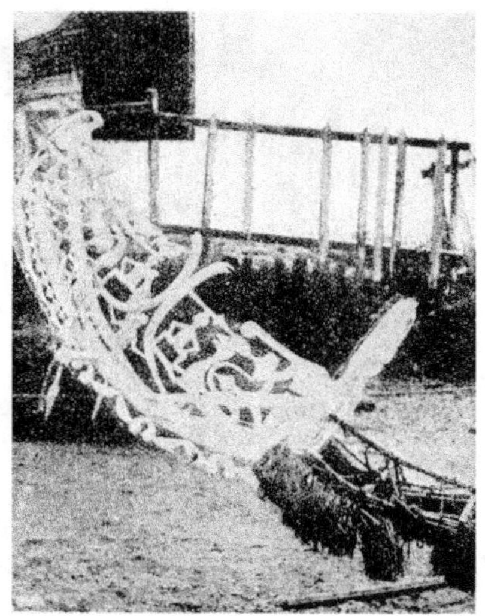

PROW OF A WAR CANOE.

MAPS

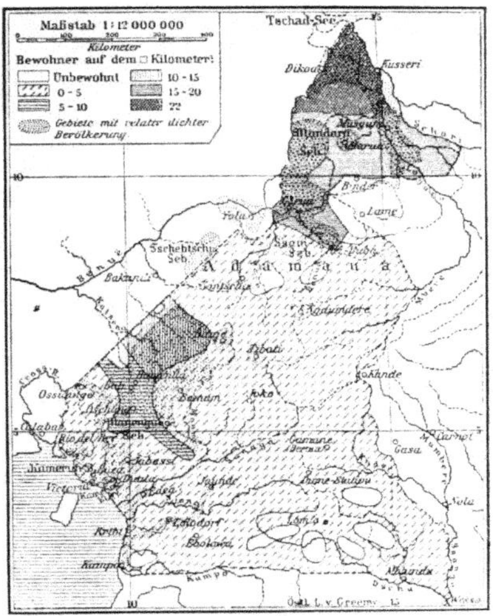

DENSITY OF THE POPULATION.

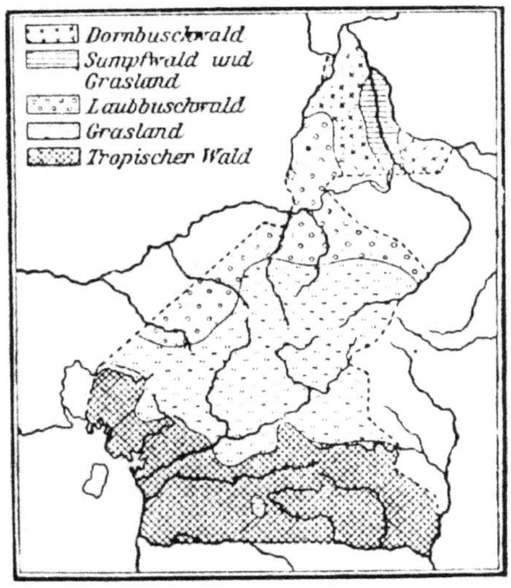

FLORA.

PLATE 194

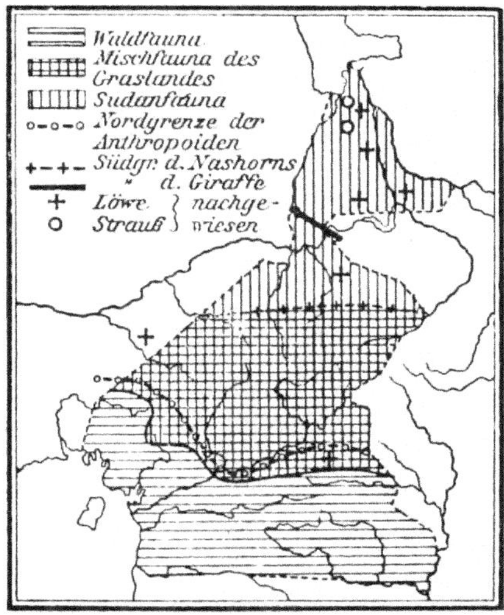

FAUNA.

PLATE 195

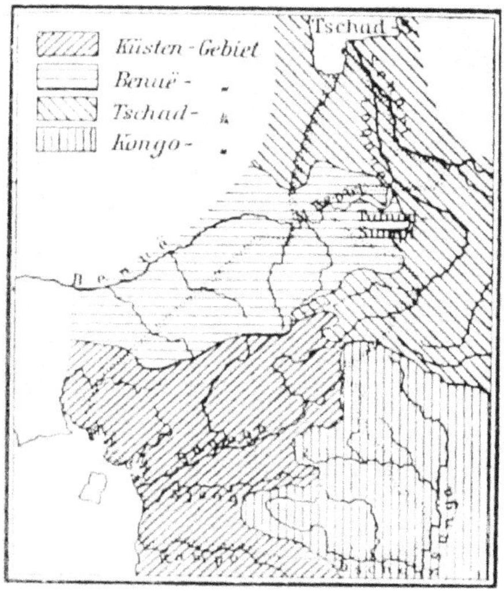

RIVER BASINS.

PLATE 196

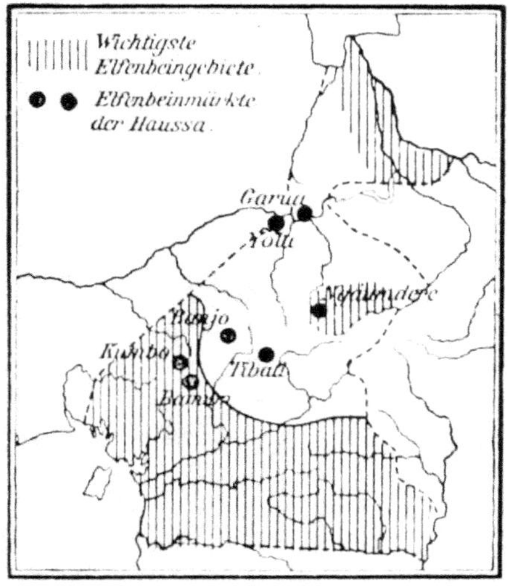

IVORY DISTRICTS.

PLATE 197

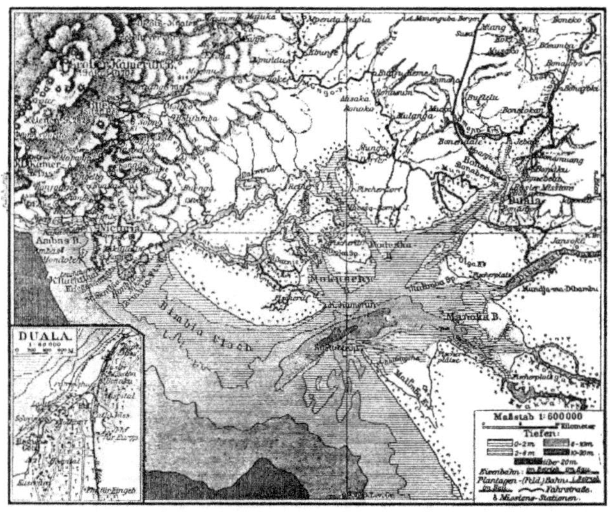

CHART SHOWING ENTRANCE TO DUALA FROM THE SEA.

PLATE 198

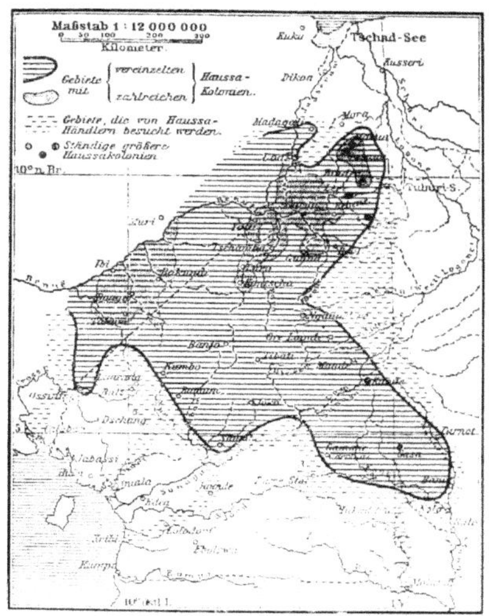

HAUSA TERRITORY.

PLATE 199

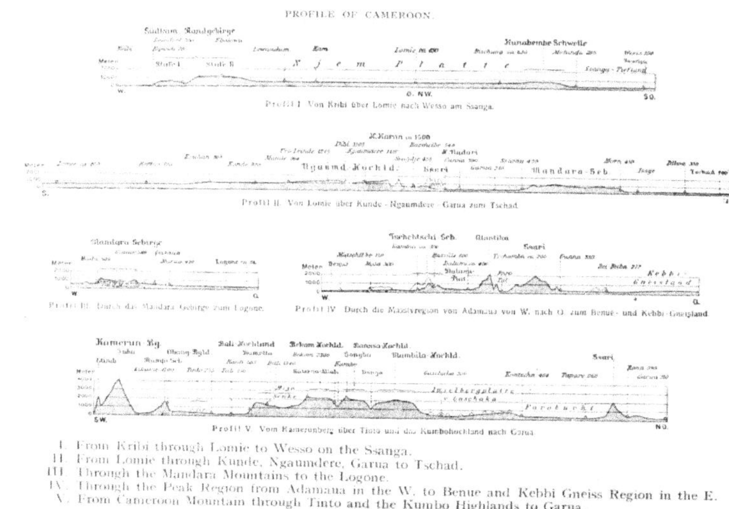

I. From Kribi through Lomie to Wesso on the Ssanga.
II. From Lomie through Kunde, Ngaumdere, Garua to Tschad.
III. Through the Mandara Mountains to the Logone.
IV. Through the Peak Region from Adamaua in the W. to Benue and Kebbi Gneiss Region in the E.
V. From Cameroon Mountain through Tinto and the Kumbo Highlands to Garua.

PROFILE OF CAMEROON.

Profil I. Von Kribi über Lomle nach Wesso am Ssanga.

Profil II. Von Lomic über Kunde-Ngaumdere-Garua zum Tschad.

Profil III. Durch das Mandara-Gebirge zum Logone.

Profil IV. Durch die Massivregion von Adamaua von W. nach O. zum Benuë-und Kebbi-Gneisland.

Profil V. Vom Kamerunberg über Tinto und das Kumbohochland nach Garua.

I. From Kribi through Lomie to Wesso on the Ssanga.
II. From Lomie through Kunde, Ngaumdere, Garua to Tschad.
III. Through the Mandara Mountains to the Logone.
IV. Through the Peak Region from Adamaua in the W. to Benue and Kebbi Gneiss Region in the E.
V. From Cameroon Mountain through Tinto and the Kumbo Highlands to Garua.

PLATE 200

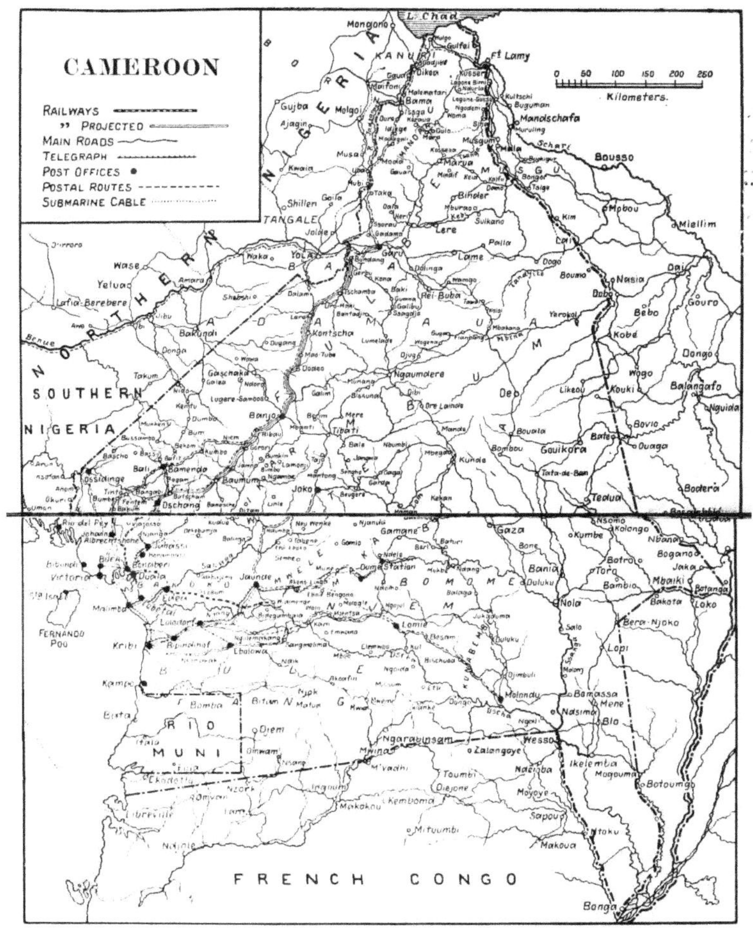

CAMEROON.

A. F. CALVERT'S MAP OF CAMEROON.

www.ingramcontent.com/pod-product-compliance
Lightning Source LLC
Chambersburg PA
CBHW071622030726
47598CB00001B/387